Whatever It Takes

Whatever It Takes

A Story of Family Survival

ELAINE LORDAN

EBURY
PRESS

1 3 5 7 9 10 8 6 4 2

Published in 2007 by Ebury Press, an imprint of Ebury Publishing

Ebury Publishing is a division of the Random House Group

The Random House Group Limited Reg. No. 954009

Addresses for companies within the Random House Group can be found at www.randomhouse.co.uk

A CIP catalogue record for this book is available from the British Library

The Random House Group Limited makes every effort to ensure that the papers used in our books are made from trees that have been legally sourced from well-managed and credibly certified forests. Our paper procurement policy can be found on www.randomhouse.co.uk

Printed and bound in Great Britain by Clays Ltd, St Ives PLC

HB ISBN 9780091917883
PB ISBN 9780091921767

To
Bernie and James
and all who loved them

Acknowledgements

I'd like to thank everybody who helped this book to come about, especially:

My sister Sophie, who generously shared many memories with me, and my dad Garrett, who as ever encouraged me in what I wanted to do. My cousin Kevin Lordan too, who's more like a brother to Sophie and me.

The friends I grew up with: Julie Douglas, who's been a tower of strength for as long as I can remember (and who also got the ball rolling on the book), and Debbie Hutchings, who shared in many a childhood escapade.

The staff at my primary and secondary schools, Drayton Park and Highbury Hill, who kindly allowed me back in to revisit old haunts.

My drama teacher and great inspiration, Anna Scher. Also the staff at her old theatre, who took the trouble to show me round so I could refresh my memories.

My great friends Kathy Burke, Tilly Vosburgh and Tonny Kerrins, who read the drafts of the book and gave me invaluable feedback.

My literary agent Sheila Ableman, who saw from the first that I had a story to tell and has looked out for me ever since. She brought in Chris King, who recorded what I had to say and shaped my words into this book – becoming a good friend in the process. (And she's cheaper than a therapist.)

Finally, my husband Pete. Without him…well, without him, I wouldn't have been able to tell this story.

Contents

PROLOGUE

Well, I See it like this...

It's not as if you get any training, is it? You don't have classes in how to cope when someone you love isn't there any more. Oh, what am I saying, 'isn't there any more'? I mean dead, not just gone away somewhere with the prospect of coming back some time. Dead. Irrevocable. The end. That beloved person has gone for good.

My mum died on the 24th of March 2005, years before her time. My baby son James died nine months later, on the 18th of December, a whole lifetime before his time. Mum was sixty-two years old, James was just over a year. Mum fell in front of a tube train that was coming into a station, James had been poorly since birth.

Those are the raw facts. One of the people I loved lived life to the full, until she was dragged down by depression. The other just had time to show his potential, a hint of his character, before his short life was taken away.

Both deaths were so sudden. I suppose if someone you love has lived to a great age, death is expected, and it's possible to feel a kind of melancholy rather than a tearing grief. If Mum had lived to a hundred, stayed in good health, done everything she'd wanted to and died quietly and peacefully with her close family around her, knowing to the last how much she was loved … wouldn't that have been more bearable? Of course. But she'd still have been dead, and I still would have wanted just one more day with her …

When a baby is born very ill, like my James, you have to put your faith in medical science – and it does achieve miracles. James had operation after operation, the best of NHS care, while his dad and I experienced a kaleidoscope of hope and despair, relief and dread. But James had turned a corner – he'd just had his first birthday and he was stable, he seemed to be thriving. I hadn't seen his death coming, any more than I'd seen my mum's.

The shock waves go on and on. They get stronger and stronger, they multiply, as the enormity of what's happened sinks in. At first you can't think of anything else but who you've lost – they're gone and all you feel is a huge, raw pain. Every waking moment you feel the agony of loss. You drag yourself through the days, going through the motions of washing, dressing and eating. Ordinary things. When you sleep, you might dream of your lost love, and for a moment when you wake everything is like it used to be. Then memory kicks in and desolation is back with a vengeance. 'Bring them back! They should be here with me!'

You've heard about grief, of course, you know somewhere in your mind that this first intensity must lessen – how could people go on living if it didn't? Everybody goes on about time being a great healer. Much as you don't believe it when people say it to you, it is true. Not that the healing means you forget, of course, far from it. You never forget someone you've loved. If that person dies, they stay in your heart and mind for ever.

Hark at me going on – 'This is how you handle grief ... ' Gather round, people. All I can say is that it's a long, long process and I'm still feeling my way. Many's the time I've felt like dropping into the void that opened up in my life and staying there, but somehow you just keep going. Something inside urged me to stick with it, reminded me that life was worth living, so I could remember both sad and happy times and look to the future.

It's not something you learn – not consciously, anyway. I know I've always loved life, relished it, met it head on. The way my mum and dad brought me up, with unstinting, unconditional love and support, instilled in me a sense of my own worth, and put me on my life's course. True, my course has wobbled somewhat over the years, what with one thing and another, and I've probably made more than my fair share of mistakes. But I feel something at the heart of me that makes me what I am – a survivor, something that helps me find my bearings again and get me back on my feet.

*

When you're bereaved, everyone means well. Close friends have a knack of saying just the right thing – a quiet word that shows they empathize and that they're in tune with how you're feeling – but without overdoing it. You just know they'll be there if you need something, or someone to talk to. And they're great at giving practical help, like getting the shopping if you don't feel up to it, or cooking you some comfort food.

Other people don't really know what to say and fill the silence with comments like, 'How awful – and so close to Christmas.' Of course they don't mean that if James had died in the summer it would have been easier to bear. They're just at a loss for something to say. I'd end up feeling sorry for them. The truth is that Christmas can be a difficult time for anyone who is suffering a loss, because it's a time for families and reflection.

What I found strange is other people's assumption that there's some kind of hierarchy in grief. 'To lose a child is the very worst thing that can happen to you,' they'd inform me, solemnly. But no one has the right to say, 'My pain is greater than yours – you've only lost a mother, a sister, a brother – while I …' If you lose someone you love, the pain is the same. At least, it is for me. I'd loved my mum with all my heart, for all my life – thirty-eight and a half years. I'd loved my son with all my heart, for all of his life – a year and five days. Two unique, wonderful, beautiful people. I was blessed to have had them in my life.

Yes, blessed. I may be 'Tragic Elaine' to tabloid reporters, who've followed me ever since I was in *EastEnders*, but what do they know? I'm not tragic. Tragedy lies in a life cut short, for whatever reason. My mum's life was cut short, and so was my son's. The tragedy is theirs – the mourning is mine.

Everyone is an individual, and their circumstances are unique. I used to talk things over with family and friends, still finding the press interest intrusive, and I felt I wanted to put the record straight, but in my own words.

'You should write about it,' they said.

That was an idea that had been taking shape in my mind over recent months, as I gradually got my head together. I knew I'd never forget my mum and my son, but I wanted to make something tangible about them. Not exactly a memorial, but more like a tribute – a celebration. Set them down in words, have a written record of their lives. I have all the photos, of course, but memories would come flooding back – an adventure here, a poignant moment there, one thing leading to another. I wanted to capture them.

I started to think back on my own life – after all, I'm what my mum and my son have in common, our lives are intimately linked. I began drawing all kinds of threads together. I began to think that yes, perhaps even complete strangers might be interested in stories that resonate with their own lives. And, without being pompous, perhaps my experiences could give some help or insight to people who face the same kinds of problems.

This is a story of interconnected lives, an account of love and death, comedy and tragedy. In my life these last two have usually been not far apart from each other.

*

Now that I had decided, I told my old friend Julie, who'd been the most insistent that I had a book in me, that I'd do it. What do I do now?

She's resourceful, Julie. She looked up literary agents on the web and didn't get much further than the As.

'Let's try this one,' she said.

'What made you choose her?' I asked. 'Why Sheila Ableman?'

Had Julie been doing in-depth research into the literary establishment, comparing and contrasting the calibre and reputation of agents?

'She's got the same name as my mum,' said Julie.

Say no more.

Julie phoned and Sheila phoned back, a meeting was arranged – and we had no idea what to expect.

'She'll probably expect us to be all business like, so you take a notebook,' I said to Julie. 'And a pen,' I added.

Julie drove us there, and as we stood outside the office she said, 'Look, I've got my official notebook.' Yeah – bright pink and spangly, borrowed from her young daughter. Very professional. At least the pen didn't have a feather on it and play tunes.

'Don't forget to look like you're taking notes,' I said as we went in.

During our friendly, informative meeting, Julie made intelligent noises and wrote in her notebook. When she seemed to be drifting off, I gave her a nudge. The meeting ended with mutual assurances of meeting up again, and Julie and I left.

'You looked good in there,' I said. 'Well, mostly. Can I see your notes?'

Julie handed over the book and I leafed through it. Whole

pages were covered in doodles and noughts and crosses. As ever, she had me in stitches.

Well, we all persevered, all did our bit, and in the end my book came to life.

Here it is.

CHAPTER ONE

Highbury Fields Forever!

All my life I've lived in one part of London – Islington. And if that makes you think of trendy media types swanning about in posh houses, think again. It was very different when I was a kid. There were always the rich bits, of course, but when I was growing up, in the late Sixties and early Seventies, things were pretty grim for a lot of people. There was real poverty, rough estates with no-go areas. Many of the grand period houses lining the streets were carved into flats and packed with as many tenants as a landlord could cram in, so they became shabby and run-down.

Not that I was ever aware of lacking anything myself. When I was little, life for me was pretty damn perfect. And in fact my family was better off than a lot of others. My dad was in steady work, and my mum was a fantastic manager who always made sure there was good food on the table and good clothes on our backs.

If anything sums up my charmed existence, it's a certain red-letter day – on a red double-decker bus, as it happens, the number 19, coming back from Chapel Market. For the first time my mum let me pay my own fare. Right, I thought, that's it. I've bought the bus. If I handed over money in shops and got things back, why shouldn't I now own the bus?

I did understand that I couldn't take the bus home, but as far as I was concerned that number 19 belonged to me. I'm not sure when disillusion set in, but for a while at least that bus made my life even better than it already was. It took me everywhere I wanted to go, anywhere in Islington – and Islington was my world. After all, what does a kid need? I had my home, with my mum, dad and sister. All my friends lived nearby, if not in the same building, and even my primary school was just down the road. We had Highbury Fields, with its open-air pool, the swing park, the pitch and putt course, the refreshment hut where we could buy sweets and fizzy drinks, and we could ride our bikes all over the place. The Arsenal football stadium was just five minutes away, and I used to love going there with my dad. There were plenty of little shops round the corner in Highbury Barn that sold everything we needed. One of them, the butcher's, had a great big model of a jolly old butcher standing outside, complete with straw boater and red and white striped apron over a big belly. He used to fascinate me as a kid, and he's still there today. And for a change there was Chapel Market a bus ride away, a busy, bustling street with loads of different stalls selling all kinds of fascinating stuff.

Wherever I've been in the world, on holiday or on tour, it was always this patch of north London that I came back to. I've moved house only twice in all this time, and even then just round the corner. Of course, it's not just me who feels rooted here. Whenever I'm walking around, I always bump into people I knew at school, who still live in the area. Whole generations of families have grown up here and never felt any reason to leave. There's a real village feel about Highbury, even today – it's got character.

It's in Highbury and Islington that I've known the best of times, the worst of times – and all times in between.

*

My first home was in one of those grand period houses. It was Victorian, built in brick over four storeys, with big sash windows at the front complete with original shutters, an arch over the front door and solid pillars on either side of the front gate. It was on Highbury Hill: number 6, on the left-hand side as you go down the hill. And I do mean '*in* one of those grand period houses' – we had a flat on the ground floor, with a kitchen, a bedroom for me and my sister, a front room that was divided into two to make a bedroom for my parents, and a shared bathroom and toilet upstairs. It had a little front garden that nobody used much, and a big back garden with an apple tree that was a great kids' playground. At the bottom of the back garden was a high brick wall, and beyond that was an even better kids' playground – Highbury Fields.

My dad had managed to get hold of the flat just in time for my débul in the world. He and Mum had been living in a bedsit with my sister (christened Sophia, but usually called Sophie), who's three years older than me, in Landseer Road off the Holloway Road. With another baby on the way, obviously the bedsit was going to be an even tighter squeeze, so Dad was looking out for a bigger place. Mum, meanwhile, was in the Whittington Hospital, on Highgate Hill, having me – and that hospital is where, years later, I would plan to have my own baby.

I was born on the 8th of August 1966, just nine days after England won the World Cup. How did the country cope with two such momentous events? My mum used to tell me that she was massive – *massive* – when she was expecting me. Hard to credit, given her trim figure and the fact that I've never been what you might call large. Apparently she had just the one dress that fitted her and kept her cool – it was a boiling summer that year. Every night she'd rinse it out and it'd be dry for the morning – and the next morning … and the next … She went to three weeks overdue. I don't think they'd allow that now.

Mum was originally going to call me Scarlett, being a big fan of the film *Gone with the Wind* and Vivien Leigh, but in the end she changed her mind and I was christened Elaine Bernadette (after my mum) Lordan, though I like to think that if anyone could carry off the name Scarlett, it's me.

Dad had heard about the flat on Highbury Hill, but hadn't been able to check it out properly. Still, taking a gamble – he's always been a betting man – he packed up what little furniture they had into a van and took it all to this house. So my mum faced coming out of hospital with a newborn baby and the possibility of having nowhere to live. Luckily, Dad managed to swing the deal, and that was our home for the next fourteen years.

There were four flats in the building, one on each floor. All the neighbours were very friendly – we really did leave our doors open. Seems like another age … A great bonus was that there were lots of kids around, nine at one point, I think. It always seemed to be someone's birthday, a great excuse for a party.

We all loved living there. The only drawback was that it was freezing in winter. Nobody had central heating back then. Getting up at night to run to the loo upstairs was a real endurance test – though snuggling back under the covers made up for it. A few years after we moved in, the tenants upstairs moved out and we managed to get their three rooms too – going up in the world! But, as I've said, we were never particularly down. Compared with today, when most people have loads of stuff, I suppose we did go short of some things – but I was never aware of it.

My dad had a good job as a bricklayer. He was one of the thousands of Irish people who came over to England to find work and get away from the poor conditions and unemployment at home. He and Mum both came from Cork, Mum from the countryside and Dad from the town, and for Dad's family especially times were really hard.

A lot of Irish immigrants came to Islington, and between them they created a little slice of Ireland in north London. Someone once said that at one time there were more Irishmen in Islington than in Ireland – and for all I know, that's true. I certainly grew up with a strong sense of being Catholic Irish. Mum and Dad may have left Cork, but I don't think Cork ever left them! They kept their Southern Irish accents too – and that's something I would have loved to have, that natural lilt to the voice. Even when my mum was telling me off, it sounded musical. I can still hear her saying things like, 'Will yer be lookin' where yer goin' now!' As it was, like all the other norf London kids, I spoke corblimey cockney. Sometimes my mum and dad would complain, 'Why do you not speak more nicely?' And I'd have the hump and shoot back, 'Well, if yer wanted me to speak posh yer should've lived in bleedin' Kensington or Chelsea, shouldn't yer.' Which would shut them up – though I didn't mean a word of it. I was very happy, for all sorts of reasons, to be living where we were. And anyway, my accent was to come in very handy some years later for a certain TV soap set in the East End …

I can put the Irish accent on, sounding uncannily like my mum, I'm told – and when I'm feeling particularly in touch with my family's roots I'll proclaim: 'Irish, but robbed of the accent!'

Dad worked hard and was very good about money. He always handed over the housekeeping, even if he and Mum had had a row, and I knew even then that a lot of men weren't like that. Mum and Dad rowed quite a lot – they were both passionate and hot-tempered, and ructions occasionally led to violence. That kind of thing may seem shocking now, but in those days it was quite common for husbands to hit their wives. Many a woman would be out walking wearing sunglasses in the rain – not to look fashionable or anything, just to hide their black eyes.

The biggest bone of contention between my parents was Mum's insistence that she wanted to go out to work. She stayed at home until I went to nursery, then worked shifts in local pubs and the odd shop to fit round me and my sister. As I realized later, it was very important to her to have money of her own. Not that Dad was ever tight – he was always a generous, open-handed man – but Mum wanted independence, the freedom to spend money on her own bits and bobs and build up some savings. I guess my dad was like most men in those days, taking the traditional view that the man of the house should bring in the money while the woman stayed at home. If a wife worked, it was a bad reflection on the husband. Mind you, there might have been a touch of the old green-eyed monster ...

There's no two ways about it: my mother was beautiful. She had sparkling dark eyes, a mass of dark hair, a wide smile and a gorgeous figure. What with her warm heart, generous spirit and quick wit, people took to her straight away, wherever she went and wherever she worked. Not that Dad had any real reason to be jealous. Mum was a flirt, sure, but she was what I'd call an innocent flirt – never anything in it, just a laugh, a bit of banter. And Dad could talk – he was a flirt himself, and could match Mum for film-star looks. If Mum looked remarkably like a young Sophia Loren, Dad looked like a young Burt Lancaster. I look at photos of them now, especially together, and realize how well matched they were. Bernadette and Garrett Lordan – nobody could have predicted they'd be driven apart, and as a young child I had no inkling of their inner sadness and regret ...

I have a feeling that when I was born, Dad was hoping for a son – don't most men want a son, at heart? But he's been stuck with me. He used to joke about being surrounded by females – even our cat Suzy was a female (she was gorgeous – a stray we adopted). If there were any echoes of the past floating around, I didn't pick up on them. Life for me as a little kid was peachy. When Mum and Dad erupted, me and my sister just had to stay out of the way until the storm clouds blew over. Then it was back to being a warm, close-knit family again, with a lot of laughs.

We more or less kept open house. Even as a young kid I noticed the difference between my mum and other mums. When I knocked on a friend's door to ask her to come out to play, and she was having her tea, her mum would usually tell me to come back later. But if I was having my tea and a friend knocked for me, Mum would always say, 'Come in, come in! Would you be wantin' something to eat?'

Mum and Dad were very sociable – they had a party most weeks, with lots of drinking, singing and dancing. They were great dancers – I have a video of them tearing up the dance floor in a fantastic rock'n'roll jive. And people were always dropping in at odd times. Now, for me, that was a double-edged sword: I've always loved getting attention, so visitors taking an interest in me were right up my street. But when it came to other people taking up my mum's time, that was another kettle of fish.

I was very, very possessive of my mum – nobody loved her more than me, I thought, and nobody had a greater right to her. In fact I used to wish she wasn't so popular. Even when I was very young, too young for nursery, I didn't like it when one of her many friends came round for coffee. I used to crawl under the table and start kicking the friend's legs to make her go home. I was horrible, really, but I loved my mum so much. Other people were always wanting to talk to her – or, as I saw it, take her away from me. So when we went to the local shops, if I saw somebody we knew coming, I'd drag her into a doorway so she wouldn't see them. 'Look at this, Mum!' I'd say, pretending to be interested in something in a shop window.

My sister felt the same way about our mum – we'd do anything for her. I remember once when Mum was ill in bed with a bad dose of flu, and Sophie and I were in the kitchen, squabbling over who'd be Mrs Bridges and who'd be Ruby the scullery maid (*Upstairs Downstairs* was very popular at the time). Mrs Bridges would be the one to take Mum something to eat or drink, while Ruby had to clear up. As I was younger and smaller than my sister, it was usually me that got relegated to the scullery.

Mum would only have to mention that she wanted something done and I'd dash off to do it. Or at least I'd try to – I was so accident-prone, all arms and legs, that Mum used to call me Norman Wisdom, and not because I wore a funny cap back to front. Mum would start asking me, 'Would ya go upstairs and fetch me–' and break off – 'No, I've changed me mind.' And I'd go, 'What, Mum, please, what d'ya want? I'll get it for you.' She'd say, 'Oh no, you'll forget there's the door, the wall, the set of stairs – you'd just be flyin' all over the place!'

I suppose I was a bit spoiled, being the youngest, and I certainly knew how to twist my mum round my little finger.

When I was older, she told me how I used to play up when I went to nursery. I would scream and cry as she left me there, and her heart would be breaking. She'd started part-time work by then, in a bar, and all through her shift she'd be fretting about me, feeling terrible. She finally confided in one of the nursery teachers, who said, 'Tomorrow morning you look through the window when you've dropped her off – I guarantee that one minute after you've gone she's got her arms folded and is organizing everybody, telling them what to do and how to do it.'

Sure enough, there were tears and drama one minute, then the next I was in the middle of the room saying, 'We're playing this game, we're doing this, we're doing that.' I guess I was just being a drama queen and tugging at her heartstrings. Well, it worked for a bit …

I myself remember another time, when I refused to get dressed. I was always particular about all my clothes – they had to feel just right – and one day my knickers didn't seem to fit properly, so I took them off and refused to put them back on. Though I did put them on my head and ran round the house otherwise naked, making a fuss and refusing to put any clothes on. My mum couldn't do a thing with me and actually had to take the morning off work. How easy-going was she! I feel guilty now, taking advantage, even if I was only a little kid. Dad would give us a wallop on occasion, or a crack over the head – there was no agonizing about the rights and wrongs of smacking in those days, it was a fact of life and most people did it. But not Mum, she was too tender-hearted to raise a hand to her girls. She was always the one for peace.

She had the softest, biggest heart and would do anything for anybody. As well as looking after her own family and giving a hand to anyone who needed it, she took care of one of her brothers, DP (short for Dennis Patrick), who'd also come over to London looking for work. He was in the building trade too, and when his joints started swelling, the doctors said it was because of working outside in the cold and wet. In fact he went on to develop rheumatoid arthritis, and he had it very badly. His hands and limbs were crippled, and he was housebound. So every evening, after cooking for us, Mum would get the bus to his flat in Holloway, taking him his hot meal wrapped up in a cloth, inside a big basket. She did this for years, and she did it willingly – I never heard her complain. Years later, when my sister and I were grown up and had learned to drive, we'd drop Mum off at our uncle's. We'd also stand in for her at weekends – me Saturdays and Sophie Sundays. But even then Mum would be fretting, feeling guilty about not being there.

I can remember only one time in my entire childhood when I felt let down by my mum, and needless to say it wasn't her fault at all.

Just before I was due to go to primary school, Mum fell

ill. She lost a hell of a lot of weight – she'd gone down to six and a half stone. Later I learned that the doctors had suspected leukaemia. It took a long time to get a diagnosis, but fortunately it wasn't a life-threatening disease but an overactive thyroid gland, which is unusual in someone so young. She had to have an operation, and as Dad was working and couldn't look after my sister and me, we were sent to Bexhill-on-Sea to stay with my mum's sister, Mary, who had come over to England years before.

We stayed for about a month, and I had to start school while I was there. I sort of enjoyed it, but I wasn't happy. I didn't really understand why we'd been sent away. I'm sure it was explained to me over and over again, but it was the first time I'd been parted from my mum, and I felt angry and upset, all mixed up together. When I was older, of course, I realized that I'd felt abandoned, though I couldn't have been more wrong.

When my mum recovered and came down by train to collect us, I didn't want to speak to her. She had a load of sweets to share with us, but I wouldn't touch them, I wouldn't look at her. I totally blanked my poor mother. Years later, my own baby would do the same to me – and I got a taste of my own medicine.

It was while we were staying at Aunty Mary's that I began to realize nasty people lived in my world too. That not everybody loved me. Mary herself was lovely, but her husband was another matter. He had a big, fierce-looking dog, which my sister and I were terrified of – he'd hold it by its lead and laugh at us. And he had a horrible trick. He used to get hold of Sophie and me by the ear and twist it if we said 'ain't'. He used to drag us around the room saying, 'What is the word you should be saying?' With our ears going bright red and really hurting, we couldn't think of another word – we were cockneys and that was the way we spoke.

Cold, calculated cruelty, that's what it was. When our dad walloped us, my sister and I both knew that it was in the heat of the moment – over almost before it began – and in any case we deserved it because we'd been naughty. As kids, we understood that. Our uncle, on the other hand, enjoyed tormenting us – pretending to correct our grammar. What a dodge-pot. He's dead now, and I can't say I'm sorry.

Still, apart from dubious relatives-by-marriage, I do know now just how lucky I was to have the kind of childhood I did. Unconditional love from both my parents was the bedrock of my existence. Whatever it is that's helped me survive the later troubles of my life, I'm sure it was rooted in that love, that security.

I'm sounding very serious now. Of course I'm seeing things from an adult's perspective. As a child – and a hot-headed, madcap one at that – having parents who loved me, and who I loved with all my heart, was just the most natural thing in the world.

That's not to say that other people weren't important in that world. There was my sister Sophie, of course. We often fought like cat and dog, as sisters do, and the three-year age gap made quite a difference at first. But we basically loved each other dearly and became good friends, which we remain. Like me, Sophie still lives in Highbury, just a five-minute walk away from my place.

Then there was the wider family. Both my mum and my dad came from big families – they each had four brothers and two sisters – so there were a lot of uncles, aunts and cousins, some living in London, some back home in Cork. As well as her sister Mary and brother DP, Mum's brother Jerry (his full name was Jeremiah, but nobody ever called him that) came over to the UK to work. And of course there were our grandparents, and it was quite an event when they came to stay.

We used to go to Ireland every summer for part of the six-week school holiday and stay with both sets of grandparents. My mum had grown up with her family, the O'Regans, in Enniskeane. They had a tied cottage – my grandad was a farmhand and they lived rent-free on an estate owned by a rich family. It was a tiny place for such a large family, with just two rooms downstairs, two rooms upstairs, no running water – you had to walk to the standpipe – and no inside toilet, just a hut in the middle of a field.

What a change for a couple of city kids used to the noise, bustle and lights of London! But Sophie and I adapted, as kids do. In fact I used to like the dark nights. I especially liked it when one of the uncles picked us all up in his car, and off we'd go in the twilight along little winding lanes to the nearest pub. There wasn't a lot else to do in that part of the country in those days, and I'm not sure things have changed much since. Us kids would have lemonade and crisps while the adults got noisy and convivial at the bar. There was always a lot of drinking and a lot of singing. My dad had a fantastic voice – he could easily have been a professional.

During the day we'd often go the beach at nearby Inchydoney – with its golden sands, it was a beautiful, magic place, and it's still unspoiled to this day.

I got on especially well with Grandad O'Regan. He was a lovely, gentle man. I can see him now, sitting there in his little rocking chair, a trilby perched on his head. I remember once I'd been going through my mum's jewellery box – she always liked nice things – and I fished out a gold clip-on earring. This I promptly attached to Grandad's ear so he looked like a pirate – as much as he could wearing a trilby anyway – and the dear man put up with it, still rocking away on his chair …

Mum's family kept chickens and grew a lot of their own food, so while money was short, they managed to live quite well. It was different for Dad's family. They lived in the town of Clonakilty, about fifteen miles away. Clonakilty's chief claim to fame is that the great Irish patriot Michael Collins was born nearby, and today the town is quite a tourist attraction. But when my dad was growing up there, times were hard. His dad, my grandad, could turn his hand to anything that would bring in money.

I loved my grandparents and aunts and uncles, but when they used to come over from Ireland to stay with us in Highbury, they'd greet me with, 'Hallo, child' – which at the time I thought was really uncool. My mate Debbie's nan always used to say to her, 'All right, babe?' And I just wanted to be called babe. Looking back now, though, I can see that it was cool having Irish grandparents.

Talking about my mate Debbie brings me to another part of my world. While your family are always with you, sometimes it's friends you need – in good times and bad.

Debbie was my best friend for years, ever since we were babies. She's nine months older than me, and lived in a flat next door to ours, at number 8 Highbury Hill. Her mum Maureen and my mum were best friends themselves, so it was natural for Debbie and me to grow up more like sisters. We shared the same friends and went to the same schools. Our primary school was Drayton Park, just a short walk to Arvon Road, near the overland railway station, with its dinky little building that looks like a country cottage.

I was following my sister Sophie to this school, though originally Mum and Dad applied to send her to the nearby Catholic school, St Joan of Arc's, in Northolme Road. It was full, though, so Sophie went to Drayton Park. By the time a place came up at St Joan of Arc's, Sophie was happily settled, so Mum and Dad saw no reason to move her. And how glad was I! I loved Drayton Park – every day was an adventure, there was always something exciting to do. Even if I was ill and Mum said I should stay at home, I was still determined to go.

The school seemed big to me when I was a kid. I don't suppose it had changed much since the Fifties, or even earlier. I remember things like the old sink in the classroom where we rinsed our brushes and mixed our paints. It had a wide wooden surround, and the front was screened by a bit of curtain strung on a wire. Then there was the assembly hall, its parquet floor scuffed by thousands of feet over the years, and long wooden benches pushed against the walls. There was an old piano, which used to be played by Miss Bell, the music teacher, and, what was more wonderful, the apparatus. For climbing on, that is – a contraption that swung out from the window wall and was secured in a hole in the floor. It had upright bars and rungs, and we spent many happy hours clambering all over it.

Outside in the playground there was another structure for climbing and playing on, a big concrete tunnel. I don't know whose bright idea it was – perhaps we were supposed to play trains in it? – but at least once a day some kid would slip and crack their head on it, especially when it had been raining. No one paid much attention to Health and Safety in those days. Years after I left it was replaced by a big wooden boat, and every time I go past the school now there are masses of kids climbing all over it and having lots of fun.

Talking of cracked heads reminds me of our trips to Highbury Pool. The floor in the cafeteria was always getting wet, and hardly a week went by without someone slipping and getting concussion. We used to go regularly with the school, and as often as we could by ourselves too. It was an old-fashioned open-air pool then, and we loved it – I learned to swim there.

The pool was pretty skanky in those days; it was already half a century old by the time we started using it, and it hadn't been very well maintained. I dread to think what was lurking in the water. The pool has been redeveloped now, covered over and with all kinds of leisure-centre stuff like a gym and sauna. The changing rooms are a vast improvement on the ones we had, which were very basic wooden cubicles around the pool. They were ill-fitting, to say the least, and the boys were always trying to sneak a peek. One day, Debbie and I came across a boy who seemed to be drying himself very vigorously. We didn't know about wanking then …

Back at Drayton Park we were lucky to have great teachers. They were inspiring and encouraging, even if the odd one had a habit of throwing the blackboard rubber to get your attention – you soon learned to duck. The school had a really friendly atmosphere and I felt confident there.

There was one occasion when the school got it wrong, though, and we were lumbered with a teacher who shouldn't have been allowed anywhere near kids. This woman wasn't a pervert or anything, she just couldn't keep order in the classroom. Kids soon pick up on that and take advantage of it. When kids played up, she'd grab the nearest child to her and start shaking them violently – she had really long nails and could inflict serious damage. When this happened all the other kids would start singing, 'Shakey, shakey, baby, ah'm gonna show you how it's done …'

And get this – when this explosion was over, the teacher

would burst into tears and the girls would start to comfort her – 'Ah, don't worry, Miss.' We'd all feel sorry for *her*! What a great example she was.

One day it was my turn to be grabbed by the mad woman, and this time it wasn't so funny. It was during the long hot summer of 1976, and I was wearing a halter-neck top. As she shook me, her long nails raked my back, and the sarky singing of the other kids suddenly stopped being a joke.

I didn't want to tell my mum – I don't know why, because she always stood up for me. Anyway, kids do suffer in silence, don't they? When I got home I put on a polo neck to cover myself up, and my mum naturally asked me, 'Why would you be wearin' a polo neck on a day like this?'

I didn't answer, but then Debbie knocked on the door to ask me out to play, and she told my mum straight off. Mum was at the school first thing next morning, making her voice heard. That was the end of that teacher. I don't know exactly what happened to her, but she disappeared pretty promptly.

That teacher was very much the exception, though, which isn't to say the other teachers were soft. The headmaster was very strict – these were the days when corporal punishment was still allowed. Me and Debbie were on the receiving end one day.

It was during wet play, which now sounds a bit dubious but just means the rain kept us indoors. Debbie and I were mucking around, and started squabbling ... Debbie had a very effective technique when a fight got physical: she'd kick her leg up and down in the air so you couldn't get near her.

We were in the middle of our fight when a teacher came in and caught us. We were taken to see the headmaster, and he was frightening. He caned us both three times across the hand, and then told us to sit facing the wall. We sat there, trying not to sob, and linked our little fingers together, saying, 'Make up, make up, never do it again, if you do you get the cane' – but very quietly in case he heard us.

Of course we did fall out again, in school and out, but we always made up and were inseparable.

In those days kids could roam all over Highbury – the streets were our space as much as the fields and the park. Except for my friend Julie, that is. She lived in a flat down Highbury Hill, where her mum, Sheila, still lives. Sheila was another great mate of my mum's. Julie and I got on well at school, but her dad was really strict, and wouldn't let her go out to play in the street after school. And at weekends the family would go away to their caravan, so we didn't have time together then, either. Still, our friendship survived, and we're very close to this day.

As for the rest of us, we'd be out and about in the early evenings and you'd hear all the mothers calling their kids in for their tea. There wasn't so much traffic in those days, and there wasn't the fear about paedophiles that's all over the place now. We were told never to take sweets from strangers and had heard about dirty old men and all that, and mostly we stuck together. A lot of the time we'd just hang out, mooching around the shops or sitting in the launderette. Just what was the appeal in the launderette escapes me now. I suppose it was somewhere to sit, out of the rain. And there was always the fun of putting little Joey in the drier. Joey was one of the kids we hung out with, and he really liked being tumbled around in the drier – honest! It was usually around that point that the woman attendant came in and chased us out.

We did use the launderette in a more orthodox fashion – hardly anyone had their own washing machine then. It was only a short walk away, round the corner in Highbury Barn, very handy. One of us – Mum, Sophie or me – would take the family laundry there, carrying it in a big black bin liner. The bin liner was all very well going there, but on the way back, when the washing was warm from the drier, it tended to split, and the clean washing would fall all over the pavement. So we had to improve things. Being a brickie, Dad could get hold of those big green bags used for carrying bricks, so that's what we started to use instead. Very sturdy. No washing machine, but a thicker bag to carry the laundry in – that's progress.

Eventually, us kids tired of using the launderette as a playground and found a Turkish café instead, where the woman used to let us all hang out and play Space Invaders. Not exactly the most exciting of times, but we liked it – it was something to do.

Other times we'd play hopscotch on the pavement – or a variation we called Soapsuds. We chalked the word SOAPSUDS on the pavement, and you had to roll the ball and get it to stop on the S, then hop round the other letters. Then you rolled the ball onto the O … and so on till you'd gone through all the letters. Sounds really quaint now.

Then there was Ball in a Sock. Yes, you had to put a ball in a sock – then hold it at the open end and swing it around, chanting:

North pole
South pole
East pole
West pole

and matching actions to the words.

We also used to juggle two balls against a wall, chanting a rhyme like:

Plainsy wore a shirt
Plainsy wore a shirt
Plainsy wore it
Plainsy tore it
Plainsy is a twerp …

Then

Uppsy wore a shirt
Uppsy wore a shirt
Uppsy wore it
Uppsy tore it
Uppsy is a twerp …

And so on and so on. Debbie and I often played Two Balls against one of the pillars by her front gate – her pillars were bigger than ours, with white caps on. When we had one of our regular fallings-out, I was banished from her front pillar and had to use one of ours. When I walk past my old home I can still see Debbie and me, playing for hours, lost in our own world. We had so much energy and spent so much time out of doors, with no TV and computer games to keep us inside. Well, we did have a TV when I was very young – a little black and white one that worked like a gas meter. You had to feed it with coins. More often than not, the money would run out right in the middle of a crucial scene – 'The murderer is—' – so we'd all be hunting around for coins. Things got especially tense if the TV conked out during the racing, so my dad didn't know whether his horse had won or not. He'd rant and rave and the air would turn blue. We rented a colour TV later on, and I remember poking around in the back with some knitting needles, trying to get Mickey Mouse out of there. Good job they were plastic! As it was, my dad caught me and I got a crack across the head for that one.

But TV was never the be-all and end-all for us, and of course this was long before every house had a computer. I know I'll sound like a Grumpy Old Woman, but I can't stand kids tap-tap-tapping away on keyboards for hours on end. Why create a virtual world when you can go out and play in a real one? I suppose it's their idea of fun, but it wouldn't have done for me.

Our idea of fun, Debbie's and mine, often got us into trouble. We got up to all sorts of things. There were the rabbits, for a start.

Debbie used to keep a couple of rabbits in her back garden. Us kids were always in and out of each other's gardens and used to share all the pets. The rabbits were lovely, sweet little bundles of black fluff. We called one Columbo and one Kojak. Pity they weren't destined to have such long careers as their TV namesakes.

Debbie's grandad had made a hutch for them out of one of those massive old wooden sideboards, putting mesh in the panels of the doors – quite a grand home for bunnies. This particular occasion, it must have been summer, as it was quite late evening but still light enough to see. My mum and Debbie's mum were busy yabbering to each other in our kitchen (at least, that was the way we saw it). Debbie and I were kicking around, and found some paint under the stairs, complete with brushes. It was bright pink. One of us had the clever idea of painting the rabbit hutch – it'd look fantastic, we agreed. Really brighten it up. So while our mums were chatting, we slipped down to the garden and painted the hutch pink.

Painted ourselves, too. When we'd finished we realized we were absolutely covered in pink paint. I was wearing my brand-new high-waisted trousers fastened with three buttons – very trendy, I thought.

'We're really gonna get into trouble now,' we said to each other.

What should we do? Owning up was out of the question. Pinching the paint was bad enough to start with, but getting covered in it was worse.

Eventually Debbie and I came up with an idea, and it's one that I'm ashamed of to this day. Someone else would have to take the rap, and the obvious person was a small boy called Guy, who lived in a flat in Debbie's house. Not to put too fine a point on it, Guy was a bit ... odd, and was always being blamed for something. Well, we reasoned, with all the charity and understanding of young kids, it won't make much difference to him to take the blame for one more thing, will it?

So off we squealed to our mums.

'We were just playing with the rabbits and didn't know there was all wet paint over the hutch,' we said, wide-eyed. Yeah, right.

Poor Guy was accused – 'What on earth made you paint the rabbit hutch?' demanded two angry mums. He denied it, of course, and Debbie and I felt guilty. Not too guilty, though – we got away with it.

Mind you, we had our comeuppance. When Debbie and I went to play with the rabbits the next morning, we found them stiff as a board, lying on their backs with their little legs in the air. The paint fumes had killed them. Columbo and Kojak were no more.

Now we felt even more guilty and upset, but not enough to own up.

Another of our escapades that sticks in my memory was during the six-week summer holiday, when we were about nine or ten – anyway, still at primary school. One of my nans was over from Ireland, and Debbie and I asked her to lend us some money. Which, being kind and unsuspecting, she did.

We were going Up West. We'd heard a lot about it, and decided we'd check it out for ourselves. We got on a bus, along with our little pet dog – he was Debbie's really, but like the rabbits we shared him. He was called Hutch (we must have had a thing about American TV detectives. Though I do remember a game we played involving a home-grown cop – one we called 'Sweeney'. One of us would be Regan, usually standing at the top of the stairs and yelling, 'You slag!' The other would be that slag, yelling back, at which point there would be a chase … but I'm wandering off).

The bus took us to Piccadilly, and Debbie, me and Hutch ended up in some sort of amusement arcade. We hung about, watching the action, such as it was, and after a while realized that a couple of policemen were looking at us. We tried to look unconcerned, but they soon came over and asked, 'Who are you with?' So we pointed out a couple who happened to be standing nearby and said, 'We're with them.'

The policemen went over to them and soon came back when the couple, naturally enough, said they didn't know us, so we had to own up. 'We're by ourselves,' we said. They took us to the police station and we had to give them all our details. Neither of us had a phone at home, but we knew the name of the pub where both our mothers were working, in Fenchurch Street, so the police phoned them.

They couldn't come and pick us up till after their shift, so the police were left wondering what to do with two little girls and a dog. Eventually they put us all in a cell, which they no doubt regretted as we decided to amuse ourselves by singing Lena Zavaroni songs – well, Debbie and I did, Hutch just lay down with his paws over his eyes. We were mad about Lena at the time. With her belter of a voice, she'd been a smash on *Opportunity Knocks*, and she was only about three years older than us. I don't know how entertaining the policemen found our endless renditions of 'Ma, He's Making Eyes at Me', but at least it made the time pass happily, putting off thoughts of the inevitable retribution.

In fact, though, when our mums arrived, they seemed more amused than anything else. We did get a bollocking, of course, for going alone to the West End, but no big deal. Looking back, we probably had a narrow escape, considering what can happen to kids on their own.

Another of our escapades was entirely my fault. We eventually got a phone in our flat, but my dad was paranoid about how much the calls were going to cost. As a precaution, he got one of those money boxes in the shape of a little red telephone box, the old-fashioned type. Every time you made a call, you had to put the money in. Well, one day the funfair came to Highbury Fields – and rides don't come cheap. Debbie and I soon spent what we had, but really wanted more rides, so I went back to our house and raided the telephone box. Debbie and I had a great time, and like a kid I just closed my mind to the consequences.

The next day, when my dad noticed how light the box

was, the recriminations came thick and fast. Dad blamed Mum's brother Jerry, who by now was living and working nearby and used to visit us a lot. Jerry was drinking heavily at the time, and was known for being a bit of a rogue – a charming, lovable, handsome rogue, mind you – so he made a handy scapegoat. My mum was crying, saying, 'Jerry wouldn't do that.' She was right, of course, but with all the screaming and shouting and aggro, I was just too frightened to bring it all down on my head. Mum even said to me, 'Please, Elaine, if you've taken the money, could you not just tell me?' And still I kept schtum, so poor Jerry got the blame. I did own up eventually, but not until years later, and the guilt has stayed with me ever since.

Meanwhile, our horizons began to expand. As well as our regular trips to Ireland, one year we went on holiday to a Warner's holiday camp on Canvey Island in Essex. Not the most beautiful place in the world, I must admit, but it did give us all an indelible memory.

There was a Tarzan competition. The men had to get up on to a diving board, give a Tarzan call – 'Aaaah-ah-ah-ah' – while beating their chests with their fists, dive in the pool and swim a length. My dad, up for anything, entered, undeterred by the fact he couldn't swim. Up he got on the top board, cutting a fine figure. He wasn't a big bloke, but he was well built, muscular from all the hard physical work he did. He duly let rip with the old jungle cry – and afterwards everybody agreed his call was the best ever. However, he then jumped into the pool – he couldn't dive any more than he could swim – and proceeded to drown. At which point the lifeguard jumped in and rescued him. A bit ignominious, but at least he gave it a go.

When I was ten, our holidays went upmarket – to Spain. Our first trip abroad, but not before some lively discussion about passports.

'Garrett,' said my practical mum, 'do you not think it would be better for the girls if they had British passports?'

Thunder from my dad. Slamming his fist on to the kitchen table to emphasize each syllable, he bellowed, 'No feckin' child of mine will ever have a feckin' British feckin' passport!'

My dad had had to come to England for work, but the prejudice he'd met in those early days had left its mark. This was the time, remember – the late Fifties – when a landlord could put up a sign in the window that brazenly said, 'No Blacks. No Jews. No Irish. No Dogs.'

Dad was always bitter about this – and the way his strong accent was mocked (saying 't' instead of 'th'), and being called Paddy. He softened later, but things still rankled at the time. I'm sure he would have gone home if he could, but not without my mum, and she wanted to stay put. Their separation wouldn't come about until years later.

In the end Sophie and I got Irish passports, and very handsome they were, too, in a nice green cover with a beautiful Irish harp picked out in gilt. I was thrilled – I'd made a special effort for my passport photo, plaiting my long hair and brushing it out so it would look thicker. All the official writing was in three languages, Irish Gaelic, English and French. As the passport said, my eyes and hair were dark brown, my face was oval, and – I love this bit – under 'Height', I was 'growing'. At least I didn't have any comharthai faoi leith ('special peculiarities', if you ever need to say this in Gaelic). To this day my sister and I travel on Irish passports.

On that first holiday abroad, we arrived in Spain all excited. One day we went to a bullfight – I know, I know, it's barbaric, and I'd never go again, but in those days it was just one of the excursions and we didn't think it was wrong. At one point, men in the audience were invited to stage a mock bullfight, riding horses bareback. My dad had been brought up around horses, so he was a natural. But when the bull came out – well, we'd been told it was only a baby, but it was bloody enormous. Of course Dad was up for it, and managed to survive unscathed.

Unlike my poor mum. Not that she fought a bull – though I'm sure she would have if she'd had to – but along with the other women in the audience she was invited to compete in an obstacle course around the ring. 'Go on, Bernie, go on,' said my dad. Mum wasn't keen, but Dad kept on at her, and before she knew it Mum was volunteered and off she went, jumping fences like a good 'un. Until one particular fence – a high one. She got stuck on the top, and couldn't go forwards or backwards.

'Wait there!' yelled my dad – as if she had an option – and he bounded over to her as a one-man rescue party. 'There you go!' he yelled, both hands on her arse and shoving her over. Disaster. Mum landed awkwardly, hurting her arm badly. The pain got worse, so after a hoo-ha with the holiday rep and talk of insurance, she went to hospital. It turned out her arm was broken and she spent the rest of the holiday in plaster. She realized it was an accident, but she wasn't best pleased – and Dad was uncharacteristically quiet …

*

So there they are, my first ten years. Family life revolving around the home and our neighbourhood, Mum and Dad rowing and reconciling. School for me and my sister, playing out with our friends. Breaking up and making up. Regular trips to Ireland to see the relatives, and the odd excursion abroad. Birthdays, Christmases – and Holy Communion. Mustn't forget that. When Sophie and I had our first Holy Communion, like all the other Catholic girls we looked like miniature brides, wearing a long white dress and a veil. Mum and Dad were so proud of us.

They'd sent Sophie and me to St Joan of Arc's Church in Highbury Park on Saturday mornings, to prepare for our first communion. It's not a particularly striking building from the outside, but it's absolutely beautiful inside. I quite enjoyed my instruction, though I can't say I've been especially observant since. There's another reason that church has a special place in my heart. Every time I go past it, I remember the service held there for my mum's funeral, and I cling to the beauty of it.

But that day was to be years in the future. Nothing at the time really cast much of a cloud on my privileged childhood. I racketed around, a healthy, energetic little kid, who had everything she wanted, who lived in the best place on earth to realize her dream. Because even then I had a dream.

I was so thankful that my mum and dad had settled in Islington. They might have chosen other places that were popular with Irish immigrants – Shepherd's Bush, say, or of course Kilburn. Great places both, I'm sure, with a lot going for them. But they didn't have the one person who was to transform my life, the woman who would be second only to my mum in her influence on me. She set the course of my life and made my dream – to be an actress – come true.

Anna Scher.

CHAPTER TWO

Scher Genius

I've always wanted to be an actress, ever since I was a little kid. This will come as no surprise to anybody who knows me. My mum used to say that I was performing the minute I opened my mouth. I don't know where I get it from – there were no theatricals in either my mum's family or my dad's. A lot of drama, true, and a hell of a lot of characters, but that was real life. While my dad and his brothers enjoyed singing in pubs and at parties – and very good they were too – there was never any question of the professional stage, of earning a living as a performer.

I, on the other hand, can't remember ever wanting to be anything else, not really. Though I did have a phase of wanting to be a cleaner. I've always liked things tidy, and in our Highbury Hill flat, the mantelpiece in the living room really used to drive me mad. My mum piled up all sorts of stuff there, it was really cluttered, and I was itching to sort it out. When I was older, I used to iron my money (the notes, anyway), so there was probably a touch of the obsessive compulsive hovering about me. But the cleaning ambition soon evaporated as the acting bug grew stronger.

Anything could spark off a performance. I remember seeing a film on our little black and white TV – the one with a meter that we had to put money into. It was some old costume drama, and one scene in particular struck me. A woman wearing an old-fashioned headdress dashed into a church, shouting, 'Sire, Sire, come quickly – we need you!' After that, I ran around the flat for weeks with a tea towel tied to my head, yelling, 'Sire, Sire, come quickly – we need you!' Despite having no idea what a 'sire' was. What my parents had to put up with …

I used to tell everybody I wanted to be an actress, whether they wanted to know or not. If I was out in Highbury Fields and saw the veteran actor Arthur Mullard (of TV's *Yus My Dear* fame), who lived nearby, sitting on a bench, I'd brazenly go up to him and inform him, 'I wanna be an actress.' The poor man was only sitting down after his walk, and I had to come and spoil his peace. I wasn't tormenting him on purpose – I genuinely thought that, as an actor, he'd be interested.

Having prattled on, I'd treat him to my imitation of his catchphrase – 'Yus, my dear' – and run off. I must have irritated the hell out of him, but he was too polite to tell me to bugger off. He did take to switching benches, though.

At Drayton Park, my primary school, the teachers realized what I was about, especially Mrs Ewart, who was brilliant. She really saw something in me, with my abundance of energy, and realized I was desperate to act. So the school encouraged my dramatic leanings. My first role in a school play was as an Old Lady, and very convincing I was, if I say so myself. After my debut performance, I was Eamonn Andrews (complete with brogue and Big Red Book) in a production of *This Is Your Life*. So young, so versatile!

When I left school, my headmistress at the time, Mrs Pinder, wrote in my autograph book, 'It's never been dull having you as a pupil!' She then added something quite serious, something that I was soon to become very aware of: 'Remember, no art takes place without discipline' – heavy stuff when you're barely eleven. Mrs Pinder used to call me Sarah Bernhardt, not that the name meant anything to me then, but I was very impressed by the fact that even after she lost a leg she could convince an audience of anything ... Sounded like my kind of actress.

*

Meanwhile, out in the wider world of Islington, something ground-breaking had been started, something that was to figure hugely in my life and the lives of many others. It was a drama club for local kids. It had started small in January 1968, with after-school classes in Ecclesbourne Primary School. Within a couple of years it had become so popular that it expanded and moved into a nearby community hall, Bentham Court, in Essex Road. It was there, at the age of eight, that I first knew it. The Anna Scher Theatre.

My mum had heard about the classes, and knowing how much I wanted to act – she could hardly fail to have noticed – she put my name down.

I was so lucky that neither of my parents put the kibosh on my dream of being a proper actress. They were always encouraging and supportive, even though they knew the acting profession wasn't the most secure job in the world. How many kids' hopes have been crushed by parents who just don't care about their ambitions? Or who undermine them by saying, 'You'll never get anywhere'? My mum and dad didn't go too far the other way, either, and never actively pushed me. I got to know kids who were living out their parents' dreams of showbiz success, not their own.

Anyway, there was a pretty lengthy waiting list – word was spreading – until finally there was a place for me, and Mum took me along to Bentham Court.

I'll never forget my first sight of Anna Scher herself. She was in her early thirties, a small, slender woman, not a lot bigger than I am now, with a wild mass of long curly hair framing her beautiful face. She had warm, kind eyes and a wide smile – she radiated something that I'd later recognize as charisma. She was vital, dynamic and passionate, a woman who'd put her whole life into her theatre.

I immediately fell for Anna. Anna! A grown-up not related to me who I could call by her first name. When I called her Miss, like at school, she soon put me right. That was typical of her – no formality, no artificial barriers. I was hooked from that minute. At the age of eight I couldn't have put it into words, but I felt I'd come home and that I'd met my soulmate. What's more, I learned that she was from Cork, like both my parents, so that was another tie to bind us. Her family moved in quite different circles, though. Her dad was a dentist and expected her to do something respectable when she left school – a convent school, by the way, where Anna had the distinction of being the only Jewish girl. Anna had acted professionally as a child, and loved it, but her father forbade her to take it up as a career. They compromised on a teacher training course in music and drama – and Anna found she loved teaching too. So her Islington theatre combined her two loves.

I was with Anna's theatre for the rest of my childhood, into my teens and beyond, and we've never lost touch. Anna's students stay devoted to her. She showed us a different world, a way out of an environment that was great in a lot of ways, but limited in others. There were rocky times ahead for both of us, but when we first met, our troubles were far in the future. For now, I was starting out on an incredibly exciting adventure – at 15p for an hour and a half, twice a week after school. Value for money, I tend to think.

The big thing about Anna's theatre is that she never meant it to be a standard stage school. It wasn't about teaching well-spoken young people to become professional actors – far from it. What she was doing was so much more.

For a start, she was taking kids in off the street, perhaps to keep them out of trouble. Not that my mum would have thought of me as a street kid! But we were a world away from formally educated, middle-class types. Anna's aim was to enrich the whole person, not to aim blindly for professional acting success. And as for the word 'star' – forget it.

She hated the whole idea of stardom. She wanted to help kids grow emotionally and intellectually, to gain confidence, express themselves articulately and think about the big issues.

Behind everything there's Anna's personal philosophy – it's all about peace, love and understanding. She mixed with people like Desmond Tutu, and told us about heroes like Martin Luther King and Nelson Mandela. She talked about morality, the difference between good and evil and the importance of truth and justice.

If all this makes Anna sound like an earnest do-gooder, nothing could be further from the truth. We all had a ball. She's always had huge energy and a wild sense of humour – she loves to laugh. She inspired us all to be curious about the world and explore it. We shouldn't think that classical music wasn't for the likes of us, or that we'd never understand great literature. She introduced music into our classes and festooned the room with literary quotations, she encouraged us to talk about things, to argue – and to listen to the other person.

In fact, the first thing new students had to do was just that – listen, and learn how to be a good audience, while other people held the floor. For someone like me, itching to get up and get stuck in – and, let's face it, show off – it was difficult, but it was great experience and useful discipline.

'Discipline' – now there's a word not often applied to me. Mrs Pinder had known that's what I needed, and most of the teachers at my next school would think I was incapable of it.

But when I knew it mattered, that it wasn't making me do something just for the sake of it, for the look of it – I was all for it. It's petty, pointless little restrictions that make me mad. Anna's insistence on discipline might seem odd, seeing as how her classes were essentially based on improvisation, but, as she demonstrated time and again, discipline and self-expression are complementary. One without the other leads to self-indulgence and takes us away from the truth of a thing.

As she taught us, everything comes from within, from within our own personality, our own experience of the world, our own perception of other people's behaviour. That meant we should speak in our own words, as we spoke at home and among ourselves. And we learned how to move as naturally as we spoke.

We started with quite simple exercises. One of Anna's favourite props was a little red box with a phone on it. She'd say to one of us, 'When the phone rings, pick it up. You'll be told bad news or good news – and you have to react.' So she'd ring a bell, as if it was the phone going off, and as the student picked up the phone Anna would tell them the kind of news they had to respond to. So it was a question of 'Wow! That's great!' or 'Oh no – that's terrible!' She'd also put a metal chair in the middle of the floor and say, 'You're going to sit on the chair and the metal is hot. What do you do?' Then of course the chair would be cold, and you'd respond to that.

The exercises may sound simple, but they made you think and stimulated your imagination.

We progressed to more challenging scenarios, when Anna would explain the context and assign character parts – and you were off. You might be a mum telling her teenage daughter she couldn't go out, or a teenage daughter yelling back at her mum. Snippets from life, made into drama. Then more complex scenes, feeling our way along as we went, testing ourselves.

Anna's written lots of books about her philosophy in drama, and the title of one of them, written for children, just about sums me up: *Desperate to Act*. In the book, Anna talks to an aspiring actor/actress she calls Alex, and weaves her advice into fascinating stories of her own life, along with lots of incidental knowledge of the world. I love this book – I wish I'd had it when I was a child (but I was twenty-two when Anna published it, so a bit late for me). Her approach obviously struck chords with a lot of people, as more and more students wanted to join her theatre.

As well as after-school classes in the community hall, Anna held Saturday-morning sessions on a stage outside a little wooden shack in Highbury Fields, which is now a drop-in centre for under-fives. This was very popular, too – in fact, Anna's waiting list was getting longer and longer. So much so that in 1976 her theatre moved from the community hall to a converted building on Barnsbury Road. This was to be the hub of my existence until I was twenty-two.

What a magic place! It didn't look any different from all the other tall old houses in the terrace – except that high up on the front wall, just under the roof, there was a big clock with the classic drama symbol on it: the masks of comedy and tragedy, painted in black and white. So that was telling you what to expect!

Once you went up the steps and through the front door ... it was another world. There was no raised stage, just a big performing space, with grey movable screens around the walls. There were ranks of wooden benches for seating and lots of boxes for props. It was a bit gloomy until the lights – strung up all over the ceiling – came on. Here is where we all learned, the Anna Scher way.

We'd have breaks, I remember, going downstairs to the coffee bar (well, there was a small makeshift bar in the corner), with its chequered floor and boxes for sitting on. There were tall lockers there too, and old-fashioned loos. We'd buy soft drinks and chocolate, and talk about anything and everything, going over our performances.

By now, Anna's students included middle-class kids, the sons and daughters of professionals as well as the bin-man. Mostly they were friendly, though to the rest of us they could have come from another world. We'd ask them things like, 'Have your mum and dad got a swimming pool?' But Anna never took any account of class, any more than she did of race. A cockney kid like me wasn't expected to change her accent, to speak BBC English – remember, this was in the days before regional presenters were encouraged – and a black kid speaking in a strong Jamaican patois wasn't supposed to tone that down, either. What was important was speaking clearly, in your authentic accent, and making sure the audience could hear and understand what you were saying.

In time, Anna's theatre had as many as a thousand members, and an eight-year waiting list of 5,000. It just goes to show what a hunger there is for her kind of education. It's an education for life, not just for acting (and I should know – I learned a hell of a lot more from her than I did from my secondary school). Lots of kids who had no intention of acting professionally were inspired by their experience to study, to go to university. Every community in the country should have an Anna Scher's, I reckon – that'd help stop kids going out and getting ASBOs!

Mind you, for those of us who did want to make a career in the theatre, Anna developed some great contacts. She never started out with the intention of being an agency, like a conventional stage school, but word soon spread in the profession. Here were kids who were natural and unaffected, without that drama school veneer. We were considered just right for plays and films that required speaking with an authentic working-class voice. Posh kids slumming it with 'Awright, guv'nor?' just didn't cut it. So BBC producers would come scouting around – and find the likes of Kathy Burke, Tilly Vosburgh, Susan Tully, Natalie Cassidy, Phil Daniels, Dexter Fletcher, Gary and Martin Kemp, Patsy Palmer, Pauline Quirk, Linda Robson, Gillian Taylforth … Quite a roll call.

Talking of Kathy Burke and Tilly Vosburgh – there's another aspect to being at Anna Scher's. You made great mates. I met Kathy and Tilly when I was about fifteen, after I'd joined the Friday 'professional' class, having got a part in a London show – of which more later. We've been close ever since, though I nearly got off on the wrong foot with Kathy. I was gobsmacked the moment I saw her performing: she was terrific, a dynamic character and a brilliant actress, and this was long before she was famous. I wanted to be her friend, and when someone told me that her mum had died young, when Kathy was only eighteen months old, I thought of a way to ingratiate myself with her.

Mother's Day was coming up, so I thought I'd ask her what she was getting her mum as a present. She'd tell me her mum was dead, and I could be all sympathetic. Mistake.

When I said how sorry I was, Kathy fixed me with a glare and said, 'Wot you sorry for? Didn't kill 'er yerself, did ya?'

Ah, I thought, no bullshit with her. And I was right. With Kathy, what you see is what you get.

*

I know I'm getting ahead of myself here, but I just want to follow through on Anna's story. I wish I could say that she's still running her own theatre in the heart of Islington, but tragically things didn't work out that way.

For over thirty years she worked with passion and commitment, but in 2000 she suffered a severe nervous breakdown. Perhaps even she, with all her energy, was burned out. I'm not breaking a confidence here because what happened to her was well documented, along with the repercussions. Anna went to hospital, and afterwards needed a long period of rest and recovery. While she was away her theatre was, quite simply, taken away from her.

Anna may have run the theatre as its principal, but there was a board of trustees who administered it. Within a couple of years Anna had recovered and was her old self again, so she told the board she was well enough to return. They informed her that this was impossible as they'd appointed a full-time principal to replace her.

This was devastating. Immediately Anna's many friends rallied round and started a campaign to reinstate her. They were joined by Mahatma Gandhi's grandson Arun and Martin Luther King's daughter Yolanda, as well as Anna's long-time friend Desmond Tutu. Doesn't that speak volumes for Anna? Her enemies – and such an outspoken, truthful person like Anna did make enemies – said that she was unbalanced and unfit to hold office. This, to Anna's friends, was outrageous and unjust, demonizing her because of her breakdown and implying that someone who's once suffered from a mental illness like depression never really recovers.

Various compromises were suggested, but all of them were impossible for Anna to accept. Her name was removed from the theatre and it now operates as the Young Actors Theatre. Her support group, the Friends of Anna Scher, still campaigns for her reinstatement. Meanwhile Anna has set up her own alternative classes in a nearby church, calling it first the Anna Scher in Exile Theatre, and then just the Anna Scher Theatre. It's as popular as the original, though it doesn't have anything like the same space, and conditions are cramped.

As I say, Anna and I have always stayed in touch. She still lives in Islington, and we meet up regularly for lunch, a movie or both. I owe her so much. I always say that if it wasn't for her I'd be working in Woolies – no offence, Woolies workers, but it wouldn't have done for me. When we meet, we sometimes talk about the old days, but Anna doesn't like to dwell on the past. Now in her early sixties (though she doesn't seem to have aged a bit), she's as full of fire and enthusiasm as ever. It's a joy to know her. I'm just so grateful my mum took me to those after-school lessons over thirty years ago.

*

I'd been at Anna's for about three years when I got my Big Break. The musical *Annie* had opened in the West End, in May 1978, and the call had gone out for young girls to play the parts of the Orphans. If you're not familiar with the show, it's a feel-good story set in America during the Depression. Little orphan Annie is abandoned on an orphanage doorstep, and after a lot of adventures is finally adopted by a kind businessman called Oliver Warbucks. Great songs, a lot of tugging on the heartstrings and a happy ending – what more could an audience ask for? This production starred Stratford Johns as Warbucks, and Sheila

Hancock as Miss Hannigan, the mean matron of the orphanage.

Two of us from Anna Scher's were asked to go to the audition – me and another girl called Sarah. My first professional audition! And in the West End, at that. I was really keyed up, bursting with excitement.

Sarah and I were accompanied by a chaperone, a wonderful lady by the name of Maureen MacDonald, who got us to the theatre, the Victoria Palace in Victoria Street, in good time. It was going to be a long day, with at least five separate auditions in all.

As Sarah and I waited our turn, we realized we were probably the only kids who weren't from stage school. Everybody else seemed really posh – or at least they sounded like it – and looked confident. More than we did. To add to our nervousness, there was the mere fact that this was a musical. At Anna Scher's we'd listened to music, of course, and occasionally sung, as well as learning to move – but that was a long way from doing a song and dance act.

The first audition wasn't too bad. We each had to start by singing 'Happy Birthday to You'. That was OK, I could do that, knew all the words. Then for the next audition, we had to sing another song – and to my horror I realized that the stage school kids had brought along sheet music. When it was her turn, one posh kid burst into 'If I Had a Talking Picture of Yew-hoo', including a lot of arm movements and bursts of tap dancing. What was all that about? She didn't seem to think she was doing anything comical, and after a final ballet-dancer flourish she stood there beaming, evidently expecting applause.

What could Sarah and I do? We hadn't come prepared. With Maureen we rushed down to the toilets to think of a plan.

'What're you gonna do?' I asked Sarah.

Nothing for it. 'I'll borrow the sheet music for the "Talking Picture" song – at least I know how it goes,' she said. 'What about you?'

I thought and thought – then remembered that at school we'd been learning the Greek 'Freedom Song'. God knows why. Very stirring piece, though. Goes something like –

A sudden dark blinds us
A chain of steel binds us
The days of Greek freedom
Are now here …

I had no idea if the musicians would know it, so I prepared to sing unaccompanied. Soon I was on stage again, and the American director, Martin Charnin, asked me what I was going to sing. I told him.

Deep silence from the stalls.

Just as I got my nerve up and took a deep breath, the director spoke. 'Honey,' he said, 'would you come over here, please?'

I went over there, and in his American drawl he said, 'Could you sit on my lap a minute?'

When I complied, he said kindly, 'Honey, I guess you'll be following that with the Chinese national anthem?'

'Um …'

He laughed. 'Don't you know any other song?'

One of the kids had performed 'Hello Dolly' – and I knew that, I said.

So there I stood on the stage in the spotlight, a small skinny kid – but with a belter of a voice. Whenever I see Charlotte Church described as the 'Voice of an Angel', I think of myself as Elaine Lordan, 'Voice of a Docker'.

I must have made them sit up and pay attention, anyway.

'Well, hello, Dolly …' I started in a tuneful bellow.

I was singing my heart out, arms rigidly by my sides, when I remembered the dance bits the other kids had done. What could I do? I'd had no training.

As I reached the climax of the song, I decided on desperate measures.

'Dolly don't you ever GO' – with one bony hip jerked out to the side …

'Dolly don't you ever GO' – with the other bony hip jerked out to the other side …

'Away aga-a-a-a-ain!' – revolving hips, hula-hoop fashion.

I must have looked like a mad stick insect trying to bump and grind, but they still didn't tell me to go away.

I thought I was sunk, though, when we all had to perform real dance steps, instructed by a proper choreographer. 'Hop step shuffle shuffle hop step,' he ordered – or something like that. Well, I could do one of those things at a time, but not one after the other ... I was a tangle of arms and legs – Norman Wisdom all over again.

What a day. After the final audition, we had to wait while the director and his mates had a confab.

Suddenly my name was called. I was one of the chosen.

What? I must be hearing things. After my misguided choice of a foreign patriotic anthem, my pathetic attempt to sing and dance at the same time, my complete inability to place my feet in any given order – some mistake, surely?

'It can't possibly be me,' I squeaked. 'Could you check, please?'

A brief pause, and then: 'Yeah, it is you.'

I was beside myself, though as my mate Sarah hadn't got called I didn't want to make too big a deal of it ... yet.

To this day, I reckon what swung it for me was the raspberry. For one of the auditions, we had to blow a raspberry in the director's face, showing our rebellious spirit, I suppose. The stage school kids managed to produce rather neat, polite little 'thpttt's. I let rip, spit and all, wiggling my hands about my head and generally giving it welly. I'd evidently made an impression.

When I got home that night and told Mum and Dad I'd got the job – well! They were so happy for me, and next day Dad went around telling anybody who'd listen. At the next session with Anna, though, I was puzzled when she didn't immediately congratulate me. After the class I asked her why. 'Oh, darling,' she said, eyes bright with sympathy, 'I'm afraid you haven't.' What? 'But they told me I got it!' I protested. 'Well,' said Anna soothingly, 'it's a terrible shame, but you don't have it.'

What was going on? I ran home crying my heart out, my hopes shattered. But later that evening the phone rang and it was Anna – a very apologetic Anna. 'Oh, darling,' she said, 'you do!' It turned out there'd be some confusion, mixed-up messages. 'Charles and I are absolutely thrilled for you!' she went on. (Charles was Charles Verrall, her husband – he helped her run the theatre.) 'You're our first to get a musical.'

What a relief. My world turned the right way up again. I hardly dared believe it, though, until Mum got a letter from Robert Fox, the associate producer, confirming that I did have the part, and setting out all the details. Rehearsals would start in September for four weeks. Although the show had already been running for months, they needed a steady turnover of kids. There are all sorts of rules and regulations about employing child performers, as they can only work for a certain number of hours a week and weeks in a year, so each role had to alternate between a number of actors. I'd be working three days on, three days off, and earning fifty quid a week for my performances. I was seriously impressed.

I got my licence from the old Inner London Education Authority in early October – it makes me laugh now, to think that I was licensed for entertainment. It set out the maximum hours for work each day, and so on and so on, though if it'd been up to me I would have worked till I dropped. Because I loved it all – it was what I was made for. To see my photo outside the theatre, to see my name in print in the programme – fantastic! I've still got that programme. I'm one of the girls playing Pepper (my mum said that name was highly appropriate for such a hot-head), and I have to smile when I look at my brief biography, where I declare, 'When I grow up I would like to be an actress …'

My first stint on the show, which was from the end of October to the end of January 1979, was the most exciting experience of my life. Which isn't to say it wasn't hard work. It was. The hardest thing for me was the dancing – if I'd been as good at that as I was at blowing raspberries, it would've been a breeze. While even the little kids playing the younger orphans happily hopped, stepped, shuffled and turned right on cue, complete with arm movements, I must have been the choreographer's greatest challenge. God bless Peter Walker – the man had the patience of a saint. Even gave up his lunch hours to put me through the routines, again and again and again … And in the best showbiz tradition, by opening night I'd cracked it, with Peter's unfailing help and dedication, of course.

Talking of opening night, one thing had been worrying me, apart from getting the dance steps right, that is. By now I knew that actors had flowers delivered to their dressing room before curtain up – would I get any? I'd mentioned this to my mum, quite casually saying, 'Apparently, actors get flowers on opening night …' 'D'they really?' she'd say. 'That's a silly thing to be gettin'.'

On the night, in the big dressing room shared by the child actors, I saw kid after kid getting bunches of flowers, complete with cards and ribbons … would I be the only one not to get any?

As it happened, I was the very last to get any – not that Mum had planned it that way. Of course she'd never let me down. She'd been the most wonderful support during rehearsals, taking me to the theatre and going on to work, then coming back to pick me up later and listen to all my yabbering. I'd hoped my mum had been teasing, and sure enough she'd done me proud. I was so relieved – getting my bouquet meant I was a proper actress. I got good-luck telegrams, too, which I stuck around my mirror in the approved fashion.

I went on stage in a kind of happy glow, dressed in my costume of orphanage-kid pinafore and boots, my long hair in messy braids, and had a magical evening. I was twelve years and two months old, and when I sang along to one of the show-stopping numbers, 'You're Never Fully Dressed Without a Smile' – I meant it!

*

As I say, left to myself I would've gone on in *Annie* until I was too old to play an orphan, but because of the rules and regulations I had to leave at the end of January 1979. I really enjoyed my run in the show, and made a lot of friends. People I knew saw the show – especially around Christmas – and it was great that they liked it. I was especially chuffed when Mrs Pinder, my headmistress at Drayton Park Primary, sent me a note, which I still treasure: 'If you remember, I predicted one day that I would hobble up to the stage door, an old lady, to get the star's autograph – you!' (Don't know about the 'star' – but at least she didn't have to wait till she was old.) It really meant a lot to me that she came, as Mrs Pinder was one of the first people at school to see something in me.

I was asked back to *Annie* later that year, but by then I was working on a film and couldn't make it – I'd used up the time a child performer was allowed to work. I did do another stint in the show, though, starting in May the next year, and I took the precaution of practising my dance routines over and over again. I'm happy to say that at first rehearsals, Peter Walker was gobsmacked. He must have been expecting me to be as all-over-the-place as I was at the start.

I was learning all the time, and building on the foundations laid by Anna Scher. I was still going to her classes, of course, when my work schedule allowed, and she really loved hearing about my experiences. She never dreamed of pushing her students into the profession, but if that was where they wanted to go, and it happened, she was happy for them.

By the way, you noticed I slipped in 'I was working on a film'? How casual is that! I must have been so much in demand. It was actually for the Children's Film Foundation, an outfit that had been making films for kids for years. The one I was in was an adventure story called *The Mine and the Minotaur*, set in Cornwall and at the British Museum. A bunch of kids tangle with a gang of smugglers – real cutting-edge stuff! No, it was fun, a new experience after stage work, and the location was lovely.

Only one thing spoiled it for me, and that was because by now I was getting a bit prickly, a bit inverted-snobby.

It was windy in Cornwall, on the beach, and I was feeling the cold. I had a perfectly good coat of my own, but it wasn't quite up to the autumn chill. So the assistant director bought me a padded jacket, and I went apeshit. 'How dare you?' I demanded. 'D'you think I'm poor? I don't need charity!' Poor man, he was only being kind, but I felt like it was a slur on my parents.

Mind you, when Mum and Dad met me at the station, it was Dad who showed me up – or at least that was the way I saw it then. We were in the taxi queue and the driver wouldn't take us to Highbury. 'I don't go there, mate,' he told my dad, who promptly went ballistic and yelled in front of all the film people behind us, 'You feckin' must take us, yer fecker!'

'Oh, Dad,' I murmured, 'please don't.' But he ranted and raved and eventually we all piled in. Dad was perfectly within his rights, but the agony of being an adolescent!

Embarrassing parents apart, I was beginning to realize that there was a downside to my great new life of acting and getting paid for it – a downside I eventually got used to. For now, I was having just a taste of things to come.

CHAPTER THREE

'You're not on the stage now, Elaine!'

Thank you, I know I'm not on the stage. I'm in Highbury Hill School for Girls. And I bloody well wish I wasn't …

When teachers reckoned I was out of order, that was the line they usually tried. As if I was doing whatever it was because I worked on the professional stage. But I'd be doing whatever I was doing because it was me. That was what I was like. I'd be the same if I was working on a market stall instead of a West End stage. They obviously thought I was getting above myself – I had to be cut down to size. And what made it worse was that some of the girls in school picked up on this and started a campaign of bullying that could have ruined my life.

So what? Lots of kids get bullied, especially if they stick out for some reason, and I was in the public eye. More than twenty-five years have passed, so why do I still remember it so vividly? Because it was horrendous, that's why. It was wrong. A sustained campaign – I met nothing like it again until I was grown up and the tabloids got their claws into me.

I don't know if the teachers were aware of the bullying, and I'm sure I wasn't the only victim, but kids do have a conspiracy of silence. I didn't dare upset my mum by telling her everything that was going on. I hated school.

But in fairness, I must add that I remember Highbury Hill as it was in my time and as it seemed to me. Good memories tend to be overshadowed by the bad. What's more, I know people now who happily send their daughters to the school, and it's well regarded locally. But I'll never believe it was just me who was at fault.

I'd been at Highbury Hill for about a year when I got the part in *Annie*, and even before then it was quite clear that I wasn't going to fit in. My halcyon days at Drayton Park Primary were over. I'd often been told off there for going over the top, but mostly the teachers were tolerant and encouraging – at least, that's the impression I got. Secondary school was a different kettle of fish.

My first year happened to be the one that Highbury Hill changed from a grammar school to a comprehensive. There was no entrance exam so they took all sorts. I don't know, perhaps with some of the staff there was a hangover from the good old days. But I wasn't a dunce – I'd been in the top stream at Drayton Park. Perhaps they weren't used to kids like me – noisy, gobby, attention-grabbing. And, let's face it, a bit rough round the edges, with a strong cockney accent. In assembly, kids like me would look up at the sixth form, who sat apart in a kind of gallery, as they sang the school song – 'Praise My Soul the King of Heaven' – as if it was grand opera, all sweeping and trilling. We'd look at them and think, you twats. Kids like me thought anyone who stayed on at school when they could leave was an idiot. Needless to say, I know better now, but that's how I felt at the time. Hardly grammar-school aspirations!

On my very first day at my new school I got off on the wrong foot – literally. I limped in wearing odd shoes, one trendy new wedge and one platform flip-flop. And I was late, despite living just three doors away on Highbury Hill. I know, I know, there's no excuse for that, but I always left it till the last minute. The teacher looked at me as if she was thinking, we've got a right one here (or the grammar-school equivalent anyway). As ever, in my mind at least, it wasn't my fault. I had a bad foot.

At the end of that summer holiday, I'd been camping in the wilds of Wales – God knows why. I went with a youth group, along with Debbie from next door. Camping? Youth group? I don't know what got into us. Anyway, some of the other kids were pretty rough – would have made me look posh in comparison. The leaders were a trendy young couple, laid-back, a bit New Age, hey bring it on ... One evening the supper was being cooked, spaghetti bolognese in big pots over open fires. The young woman had a baby, and made the mistake of breastfeeding it in front of everybody. Now don't get me wrong – I'm all for the natural way, but the boys immediately started jeering and catcalling, 'Get yer tits out, get yer tits out!' She really should have gone in the tent.

The bloke in charge was annoyed and showed it, and one of the rough lads got the hump and kicked over the boiling pot of spag bol, which went all over my foot, and another girl copped it too. It was agony, and before long my foot was badly blistered. The woman took me and the other girl in her car to – hospital? No. The pub, where she bought us a brandy, even though we were barely eleven years old. We were grateful at the time, and the woman just said, 'That's OK, it's cheaper than petrol to the hospital.'

By the time I got home, my foot was in a terrible state, really festering. Mum and Dad went mad. Dad was always very vocal when he was angry. He phoned up the youth group office and gave them a bollocking. Meanwhile, I got treated properly in hospital – and was faced with my first day at school.

Well, the flip-flop was the only shoe that could fit on my bad foot.

*

It was at the end of that first term that something happened to make me really hate the school. Of course it seems petty now – let it go! – but if one thing makes me mad it's unfairness. Adults getting away with stuff while children have to put up with it.

Us new girls were going to be given a Christmas party, a joint party with all the other first-year classes, in the main assembly hall. For this special occasion we would be allowed to wear our own clothes – a real treat for me. I've always cared about clothes, and our school uniform was bloody awful. Shirt and tie! Skirt and blazer!

Anyway, a while before the party, the whole school was taken to see the Beatles cartoon *Yellow Submarine* on the Holloway Road. About 500 girls duly trooped there and I was sat next to a teacher. After a while I whispered to her, 'Can I go to the toilet, please? I need a wee.' She said no. Just like that. So I sat there, my bladder filling up, and I whispered again, 'Can I go to the toilet, please?' And she still said no. I sat there thinking right, I'm gonna piss myself in front of the whole school. I'm not having it, so I got up and went to the toilet.

In another hour I needed to go again (I happen to have a very quick-filling bladder). I did ask the teacher, but again she said no, the cow, and again I went to the loo anyway.

After the outing, she reported me to the headmistress. I was called in and told I wouldn't be allowed to go to the school party because I'd gone to the toilet when I'd been told I shouldn't. I was really upset. When I got home I told my mum and dad, and my dad – who was quite strict about behaving properly – rang up the school and said, 'This is a really harsh punishment – all she did was go to the toilet. You can't expect her to wet herself.'

But to no avail. So me and another girl, called Sandra, weren't allowed to go to the party and had to stay in the headmistress's office doing maths instead. Sandra didn't say what she'd done to deserve her punishment, but it was probably something really evil like farting in class.

The assembly hall was nearby, and that afternoon all we could hear was the music and the laughing and the giggling while we were doing bloody maths. It was so unfair and unreasonable, and that first Christmas was the start of me hating school.

I have to force myself to remember that it wasn't all bad, though. There were some wonderful teachers, like Mr Cairns, who taught English and liked my sense of humour, and Mr Osborne, who taught RE. I loved him – he encouraged lots of discussion and respected people's opinions. I think that's the heart of the thing – to be listened to, to be respected. Then I could respond and do well.

When I was thinking back about school, I dug out my old reports – those that have survived. I don't know why I kept them, but I'm glad I did. They do give me some sense of perspective and remind me that I could do well and wasn't a complete write-off – as well as highlighting the things that continually got me into trouble, of course.

We used to have little booklets for our reports, with a page for each subject and space at the back for assorted comments. (And mine were certainly assorted.) I would have been delighted – and so would Mum and Dad – to be told in February 1978 by my English teacher that 'Elaine has a lively and imaginative mind and works hard. She can be a delight to teach' – great! Then the 'but' – 'she does have a tendency to be intolerant towards other people'. Elsewhere I have a 'strong personality' and 'must concentrate'. Needlework reveals my dark side: 'She frequently chooses to behave very badly indeed.' Good old Mr Osborne, though, reckoned I was 'a lively and careful worker who has made excellent progress'.

The final comment in the report sums me up perfectly: 'She can be a pleasure to teach, or she can be a perfect nuisance.' No change there, then.

There were some subjects that were simply no-go areas for me, especially science, maths and art. From my science reports I see that I was never anything but 'neat'. Maths? To this day I've got a phobia. And art – as the teacher said, I had 'absolutely no feel for the subject'. One report read, 'If only Elaine showed the same enthusiasm for her artwork as she does for keeping the class entertained, perhaps she would get somewhere.' Another one said, 'Elaine's water-colours are not the masterpieces she thinks they are,' but I didn't think they were. I was taking the piss! I knew they were crap, but I kept saying they were brilliant just to be facetious. In the end, rather than endure each other, the art teacher used to get me to take her dog for a walk around the fields during her lessons.

Looking at my old reports, a pretty consistent picture emerges. I did have the ability to do well, but would rarely concentrate and showed off like a spoiled kid when I was bored. For me to persist in anything, I had to be hooked, and hooked quickly, as I had been by Anna Scher's. Then I'd be completely engaged, dedicated, and work hard. But if something didn't hold my attention, I'd drop it. Like musical instruments – I love the idea of being able to play, and I took up every instrument going: trumpet, trombone, violin, recorder, piano, guitar, everything. I'd taken music as an option as I liked the teacher, Miss Hudson, so much – she was really inspiring. But even with her help I didn't get anywhere, and after a couple of lessons I'd think, that's not for me. If truth be told, I didn't like the hard work involved.

It would have been fair comment if the headmistress had written at the end of my reports, 'Nah – she just couldn't be arsed.'

*

I did have some friends at Highbury Hill. (My sister Sophie hadn't gone there – she went to Barnsbury School and was no happier than me.) Debbie from next door went there, too, and my other old friend Julie. They were great, but I was particularly glad I had another friend to back me up – Denise, who also lived in a flat at number 6. Unlike me, she was a real tough cookie.

I wasn't particularly picked on until I worked on *Annie*, despite being small. I was always good at the verbals. But when I was taken out of school to work at certain times, that's when the bitchiness started. Name-calling, nudging, accidentally knocking things off my desk. Whispering as I went past – 'Look at her, stuck-up cow. Who does she think she is?' But I don't think I ever bragged as such about the show, or put on airs – I was enthusiastic, sure, but I suppose if someone's jealous they'll always put the worst interpretation on what you say and do.

I'd get back to my locker to find that someone had written 'slag' on the door, torn my books, or scribbled on my papers. Denise would tackle them and stand up for me, telling me they were just jealous. It was all low-level stuff at first, I suppose, but then things got more intense.

The bullying eventually reached me at home. I've mentioned that our back garden had a wall that backed on to Highbury Fields. On the other side of the wall, opposite the tennis courts, were some benches. Some of my tormentors would stand on one and look over the wall, right through the big window and into our kitchen. If they happened to catch sight of me, or I stepped out into the garden, they'd launch a barrage of insults, shouting, 'Slag! Cunt! Tart!' Jeers and shouts. I was glad I only had a short walk to school, so there wasn't much chance of getting picked on then.

When my sister Sophie heard about it she offered to help, but that only made things worse. The bullies would just jeer, 'Got your big sister to help you, then?' So I'd say to Sophie, 'Please, just leave it.'

One day after school, Denise and I walked to the off-licence down the road to get Coke and crisps. I did feel safer in her company. We must have been seen by someone who had it in for me, because as we were in the shop, a crowd gathered outside. We could see through the windows that there were boys as well as a crowd of girls from school. They were waiting.

I said to Denise, 'I'm gonna get beaten up on the way

back.' She immediately offered to stick by me, but I interrupted. 'Thanks, but don't try and help – there are too many. Just run and get my mum and dad. Please.'

Denise went ahead, shouldering her way through the crowd and breaking into a run.

As I came out, one of the girls stepped right up to me and jabbed a finger in my chest.

'Did you say you didn't like me?' she sneered.

What a question! As she was one of those who just the evening before had called me slag, cunt and tart, my only honest reply could be, 'Yeah.' Whereupon I was slapped, pushed to the ground, punched and kicked. The boys joined in too, yelling insults. I was hurting, but I managed to scramble up and run home. I've always been a fast runner. They followed me all the way. My dad was just coming out to find me, and one of the boys threatened him with a knife – I was terrified he'd get hurt. But while my dad wasn't easily intimidated, he knew things would escalate and turn even uglier if he retaliated. He grabbed my arm and hurried me indoors, cursing the mob under his breath. They eventually drifted away, but that night we got a brick thrown through our front window.

These weren't just kids behaving badly, they were thugs. Much later I learned that one of my tormentors, one of the girls, had gone on the game. Good, I thought. Nothing against prostitutes, but it's about time you got screwed.

We just couldn't seem to get any redress. The police weren't interested, and nobody seemed to take it seriously at school. It was a nightmare. I don't know how kids can get through it without help. I was lucky, I had lifelines – my family, of course, and my friends, and Anna Scher's. A great life outside school to balance it all. It was at Anna Scher's that I discovered I wasn't the only one to suffer. Some of the other kids who'd got parts on TV shows were also being bullied at school on account of it.

The bullying eventually died down, though I'm not sure why. Of course the bullies had probably found another victim, but perhaps it was when I started to fight back.

It happened because I used to go and see Denise at break time – she was in a different form from me and I'd go down to see her in her classroom. One of the girls in her class, a big tough girl, started picking on me, yelling, 'Get outta my class!' (Years later I'd be reminded of her when I heard Barbara Windsor as Peggy Mitchell, ordering someone to 'Get outta my pub!' Same dulcet tones – though, needless to say, that was all Barbara had in common with a girl like that.) At first I'd do as I was told, but one day some friends said that she was going to hit me the next time she saw me. Denise suggested, 'If you get the first whack in, that'll sort her and you'll win.'

Me whack anyone? I've never liked fighting. When girls set on me in the cloakroom, pushing me over and hitting me, I'd just curl up into a ball, trying to protect my face, my arms curved over my head – and crying. I could never project a tough image myself. I remember when Denise and I were once coming home from Petticoat Lane, both wearing heavy boy's-type shoes, fashionable at the time. As we joined the queue at the bus stop, I could see a big scary girl was eyeing me up and down, sneering, flicking her eyes to my shoes and sucking her teeth. Uh-oh, I thought, she's gonna smash my face in – hurry up, bus. Fortunately the bus wasn't long coming, and as I went to get on the girl snarled at me, 'You fink yer 'ard but yer soft as a fuckin' jelly bean!' What a relief it was to hop on the bus.

Anyway, back at school this particular day, I was marched down to Denise's classroom by my mates. They were like a trainer getting a boxer ready for a fight. 'Right,' they said, 'when she comes at you and tells you to get out, you stand your ground. Just say no.'

This sounded scary. But they went on. 'And when she comes over, just whack her one. Whatever you do, don't cry – don't cry.'

I went into the classroom and was shitting myself as this big girl came over. 'I've told you before, get outta my class,' she snarled.

I was getting the nod from my support group – 'Just say no!' And before I knew it, I whacked her across the head. Then I went mad, banging her head on the desk again and again. She couldn't get a hold on me. She came out of it the worst – she gave up!

All I could do afterwards was walk on wobbly legs to the toilets, thinking, I didn't cry, I didn't cry. I was proud of myself. I caught sight of myself in the cloakroom mirror – my long hair was all mucked up and standing on end. I looked like Kate Bush.

I knew that fighting wouldn't be Anna Scher's way of sorting things out – she's all about peace and love – but sometimes a girl's gotta do what a girl's gotta do. And from that day on, nobody stopped me going into the classroom whenever I wanted.

*

I was thankful that the bullying had stopped, but other than that school was just about the same. I was the same mix of good and bad for the teachers for the rest of my time there, and they always had that 'You're not on the stage now' to get at me with.

Not that all my work outside school was on the stage. I've always had a strong work ethic – never expected anything for nothing. To earn money one summer, when I was about twelve or thirteen, I got a Saturday job, up Chap. (That's the native's way of saying up Chapel Market, by the way.) It didn't lead to a career change.

It was a curtain shop, which also had a stall outside. It was my job to set up the stall, carrying all these heavy rolls of curtain, netting and such stuff, and laying them out, then taking everything back in at the end of the day. As we tidied up, the boss sent me to a shop to buy some cans of Coke – it had been a really hot day. He gave me a can and I thanked him. 'Thank *you*,' he said. 'See you next week.' What? My payment for a day's work – a can of Coke? Talk about taking the piss. I never went back there.

My next job was up Chap again, in a shoe shop. It was

the run-up to Christmas and the place was absolutely chocka on the last Saturday – it seemed everybody was buying new shoes at the last minute. The shop was pretty well cleaned out, except for shoes left all over the place as the display stands had been knocked over in the rush. The boss discovered that I hadn't processed a credit card properly – it was the old-fashioned way, running the machine over the cards. She was not pleased. She pointed to the heaps of shoes on the floor and ordered, 'Pick them up!' Not so much as a please, and I'd been slogging all day. The old Elaine kicked in and I said, 'No, you pick 'em up.' So she told me to get out, go home. I wasn't having that, though. 'Give me my wages first,' I demanded. She went to the till and got my money, and that was the end of selling shoes for me.

Chap had a lot of shops and stalls. What next after curtains and shoes? Wallpaper. I had a mate called Linda who already worked in the wallpaper shop. On my first day, the boss informed me, 'There is a proper way to carry wallpaper. Hold your arms out and Linda will place the rolls on them. You will be able to carry eight rolls.' Great. At least I lasted longer there – a couple of months – until money was nicked out the till and I got blamed. I was innocent, and so was Linda, but I probably wasn't proving to be the ideal assistant, so it was a good excuse to get shot of me.

When I wasn't putting up with school or trying out Saturday jobs, I was roaming round Highbury with my mates, just as we did when we were little kids. We'd do really grown-up things like cramming ourselves into the photo booth in Woolies and pulling faces. Or contorting ourselves so there were just arms, legs and bums in the photos. We'd hang around the clock tower, climbing part way up if we had the energy.

We did our share of smoking behind the bike sheds, too, or rather in the little wooden pavilion in Highbury Fields and other favourite places where we congregated. I'd started when I was about eight. It made me giddy but I persevered – though I didn't learn to inhale till I was nine. I can remember when I was old enough to go to Anna Scher's on my own, I'd walk through Chapel Market, stopping off at De Marco's ice-cream place for a lemon ice cream – delicious. I'd also buy a single cigarette, for 5p. You had to remember to buy chewy blackjacks or some other sweet to disguise the smell. Looking back, it was a terrible thing to do – the smoking, I mean, not the sweets – but at the time it was bliss.

I suppose I started smoking because all the other kids did. Dad was a smoker, but my mum was what's called a 'social smoker' – just one or two at night, and then none for a week. I found this very annoying. Why bother?

Though I took to smoking, glue-sniffing was a different matter. I started when one of my mates wanted to go halves on some glue. We'd both been suspended from school for getting into trouble – we had a three-day 'cooling-off period'. Which suited us fine. Other friends bunked off to join us.

I didn't tell my dad I was off school. I'd told Mum, but she never made a big deal of it – it was Dad who would have hit the roof, so we kept it from him. He normally left the house before I did, but this time one of his building jobs was starting later. I had to put on my uniform and pretend I was going to school as usual. I hid the clothes I was really going to wear under a bush in the front garden.

So off we all went to the fields. I sniffed the glue, but didn't think much of it, to be honest. The real downside was that my sister Sophie found me out. She smelled it on my breath and yelled, 'You stupid little bastard! You've really blown it now. I'm gonna tell Mum and Dad and they'll put you in a home.'

She didn't tell them, but for a year and a half she used it as a weapon. If I pissed her off, she'd sniff the air and say, 'Can anyone smell glue? Can you smell it, Mum? Is it my imagination?' Later, I tried to get my own back. She herself had been bunking off her school, on an even greater scale than me, and I'd found out. So when she started on me, I'd innocently say, 'What did you do at school today?'

But one day she pushed me too far and I flipped. I said to my mum, 'Right, Mum, I sniffed glue, it was a year and a half ago, and Sophie's been blackmailing me with it ever since.'

This is where my mum showed her wisdom. Instead of being angry with me, she was angry with Sophie – 'Blackmailing? That's not nice, that's wrong.'

We had a bit of a chat and I assured her I'd never sniffed glue since, and that was that.

And I could say to Sophie, 'You've got no power over me now, have you, Sophe?' Sisters!

*

Another sign of the times – boyfriends, or rather the lack of them. At school there was a lot of pressure to go out with someone, and a lot of gossip if you didn't, but I'd never had much action on that front. Playing kiss-chase with boys at primary school was about as far as I'd got. There was one boy I liked, called Terry, and I remember carefully writing on the cover of an exercise book:

Elaine and Terry
4
ever
2
gether
4
years
2
come

Sweet! Didn't last, though.

By the time I was in my early teens, what with my secondary school being all girls and me having no brothers, boys terrified me.

One of the girls at school was a bit overweight, and people used to go around saying, 'She's not kissed a boy for over a year and a half!' The shame! Much to my own shame, I joined in, saying, 'Oh no, that's terrible.'

Then I went home and said to my mum, 'Oh Mum, they're all saying she hasn't kissed a boy for a year and a half, but I haven't kissed a boy for two years!'

My mum looked at me and said, 'Don't be ridiculous, there'll be plenty of time for all that.' She was right, of course, but at the time I felt really left out.

That kiss, by the way, must have been when I sort of went out with a boy. A bunch of us had taken to hanging out in the launderette again, and one day this boy pushed me against a washing machine and said, 'D'you wanna go out with me?' I said, 'All right then.' At the end of an evening playing Space Invaders in the Turkish café, he walked me to the top of my road. We didn't have a word to say to each other. We exchanged a little kiss and that was that. Not exactly love's young dream.

So I didn't have much confidence around boys. And when I was fourteen, what little confidence I had was shattered, not by what a boy did, but what he said.

I used to wander round Highbury Fields with a bunch of girls. There were some older boys, seventeen- or eighteen-year-olds, who used to hang around us. When it came to banter, I was all right – I've always been quick with words – but one of these blokes liked to pick on me, getting me into arguments and needling me. I shouldn't have risen to the bait but I couldn't resist it, so I'd reply in kind. As he was older, he usually got the better of me. He really got to me, messed with my head.

One day I was out with my friends in the fields, when he caught up with us by the football pitch. While the others went on, he said to me, 'Will you come out with me?'

'What?' I said, gobsmacked. 'Why? You hate me, you're always getting to me. Why are you asking me out?' With that, I walked off and caught up with the other girls. When I told them, they said, 'He really does like you, that's why he's been so horrible.' Didn't make sense to me, though I thought that if it was true he'd stop tormenting me, so when he caught up with me a few days later and asked me out again, I said yes.

And do you know what he did? At the top of his voice, in front of everybody, he yelled, 'FU-U-U-CK OFF!'

So he got his little triumph, and I ran home as fast as I could, crying my eyes out. It was such a cruel thing to do, and it damaged me enormously. When I heard the girls had beaten him up on the football pitch, even that wasn't much comfort.

Funny thing, though. When I was offered a TV job twenty years later, it was for a character with the same surname as him, Slater. I could only hope it wasn't an omen.

*

Meanwhile, things were changing on the home front. The house we lived in came up for sale, and as a tenant my dad had a chance to buy it for £10,000. For all Dad's efforts, he couldn't raise the money. The bank refused him a

Made for each other – Bernie and Garrett Lordan.

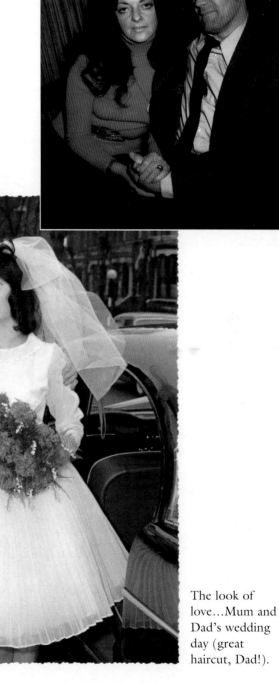

The look of love…Mum and Dad's wedding day (great haircut, Dad!).

Me aged about six, an early convert to flower power.

My sister Sophie and me, looking as if we never had a cross word.

Debbie and me, ready for our close-up in a Woolies photo booth.

Me and Debbie in Highbury Fields, playing up to the camera.

On holiday in Spain, the whole family in festive mood. Clock Dad's physique…

The Lordan family on holiday, showing just how great Seventies fashions were.

I looked lovely in white – me at my first Holy Communion, with all the other miniature brides.

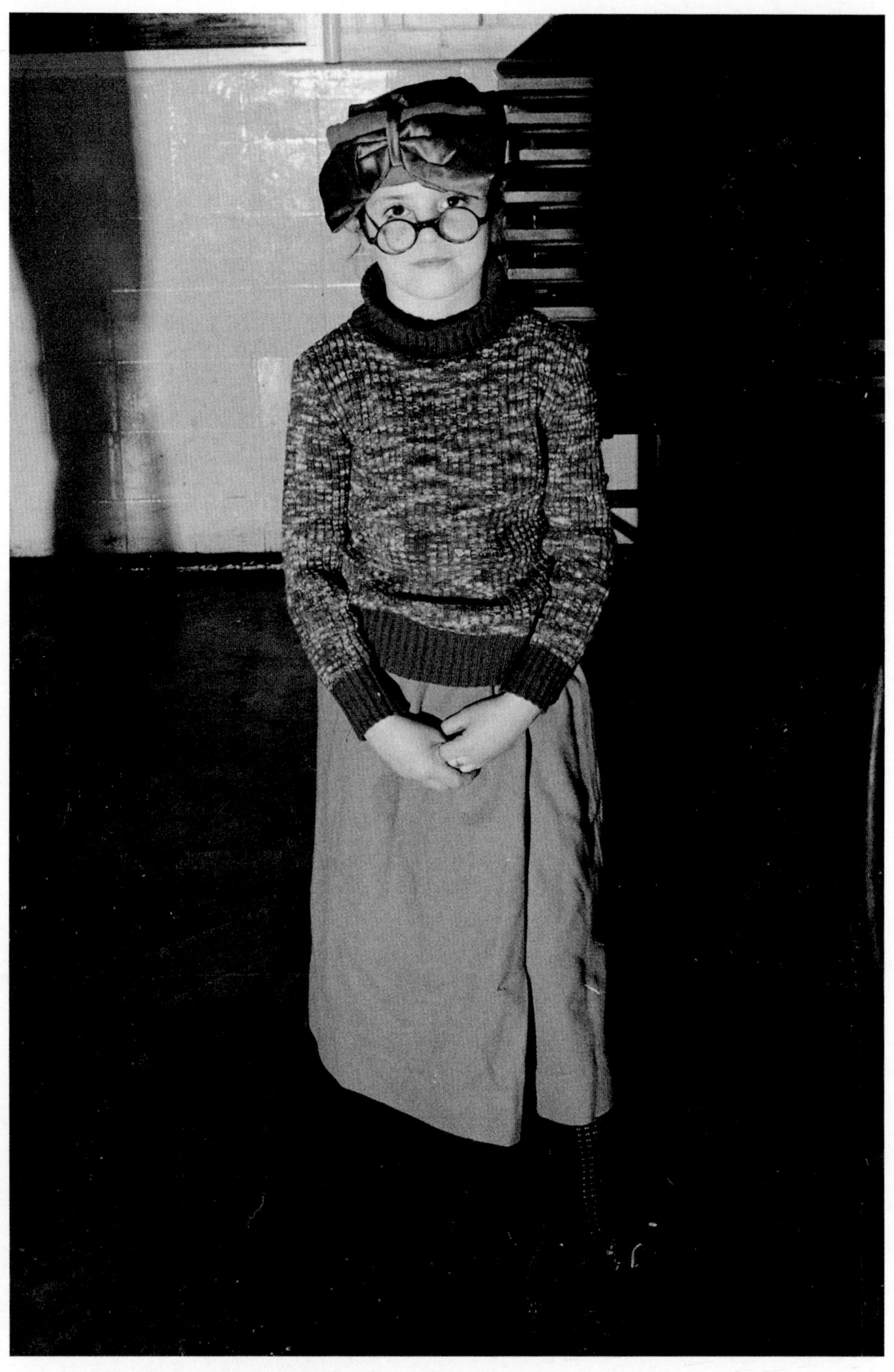

Can you see who it is yet? It's me, in my acting debut at primary school – a very convincing Old Lady.

And this is my professional debut, on the West End stage, playing Pepper in *Annie*.

The dazzling Anna Scher – my mentor and my inspiration.

My TV breakthrough, in *Tucker's Luck.* Though if I'm supposed to be Tucker's girlfriend Michelle, what am I doing cosying up to Tommy (Paul McCarthy)? Come to that, what's Tucker (old mate Todd Carty) doing with Alison (Gillian Freedman)? Bit of a swap going on there...

Me and my girls Tilly and Kathy, on one of our nights down the Old Red Lion.

A mum in a million – Bernie and me.

mortgage because he was self-employed and wasn't considered a good risk.

Ten grand! Think what it'd be worth now. The rabbit hutches in the back garden could fetch that.

Anyway, leaving the home we'd been happy in for so many years was going to be a wrench. But in fact we landed on our feet – in a council flat nearby in Highbury Grange. Matthews Court was a handsome block, built of brick not concrete, and only four storeys high. The common areas weren't that great – a bit institutional with concrete steps and metal handrails – but the flat itself felt more like a house. It was very spacious, with a big living room, three bedrooms, a fitted kitchen and a bathroom. With all due apologies to the previous tenants, the decor was lousy, but we soon put that right.

We missed our big back garden, but there were lovely views from the living-room windows – it's very leafy round there.

When I was fifteen I bought my own wardrobes – all across one wall of my bedroom, with mirror-glass doors. I thought they were the last word! I'd stand in front of them and primp for hours before going out.

While Sophie and I would move away from home in the future, and Dad would go his own way, that flat would be my mum's home for the rest of her life. She made it very stylish, very feminine – in her own image. In the living room there was the chandelier, swag curtains, an ornate fireplace, gilt mirrors, white sofas and satin cushions … Mum always liked nice things.

There was another change on the horizon for me, of course – I'd soon be leaving school. In fact, as I've got an August birthday, I was still fifteen when I left, and not a moment too soon for me.

For my last few months I was hardly at school anyway – I bunked off nearly all the time. I just couldn't see the point of it all. I sat for a couple of O levels, but refused to sit my maths CSE. When the school said I'd have to pay the £3 it cost them to enter me for the exam, I happily paid up. I would have paid a lot more to get out of it.

I really don't know why I hadn't been expelled. Perhaps it was because there was one thing I was consistently good at, which was useful to the school – swimming. I was in the school team and used to take part in competitions against other schools. I was our champion diver, no less, so I bet that was why they hung on to me. Still, I don't think they were sorry to see me go. And of course I couldn't wait to shake school dust from my feet – at the same time, on the last day of term, I was getting covered in cake mix. Or rather flour and eggs – us leavers pelted each other with the stuff. Don't know why, but it was fun at the time.

It must have been in my last report that the teacher wrote, 'It is time Elaine took responsibility for her bad behaviour ... I wonder who she thinks will want to employ her.'

Well, as it happened, someone did want to employ me. I could get back at my teachers – 'I *am* on the stage now'. Or rather, TV. BBC producers had been scouting round Anna

Scher's, auditioning for a new TV drama for kids called *Tucker's Luck*. They'd picked me, and I'd landed a six-month contract. My luck was in too!

CHAPTER FOUR

The Road to Albert Square

So I get to snog Todd Carty – tough job, but someone had to do it! I played his girlfriend, Michelle, in *Tucker's Luck*, and Todd – lovely bloke – gave me my first screen kiss. I always say he taught me everything I know …

Of course Todd had been a huge hit in the long-running kids' show *Grange Hill* – he was like a home-grown Fonz. As a kid, like everybody else, I was a fan of the show because it was so real, and because it was set in a comprehensive not a million miles from mine, though one with boys. I remember one episode when the kids were protesting about their school uniform and they turned their blazers inside out, so of course we had to copy them in our school. The whole school couldn't be punished – result!

This new spin-off series took Tucker and his black leather jacket out of school and into the world. A pretty depressing world, as it turned out – like his mates, Tucker was on the dole, and so was my character. It rang a lot of bells for people in Thatcher's Britain, in the early Eighties. Later on, Todd and I would have another TV show in common – he was

Mark Fowler for ten years before the Slaters descended on Albert Square.

Tucker's Luck was a fantastic break for me, with a part that fitted like a glove. I couldn't have been happier. I'd had some experience working in front of the camera on the film *The Mine and the Minotaur*, but TV was different, more intense, and with the demands of a weekly schedule. I also got my first taste of strangers recognizing me in the street. They'd stop me and say, 'It's you, isn't it, that Michelle Passmore off *Tucker's Luck*?' At the time I didn't know how to handle it, so I used to deny it was me. One occasion made me smile, though. Me and a mate went away on holiday to Spain soon after the show began, and two boys started chatting us up. One said to me, 'It's you, off the telly, innit?' No, I replied as usual, then his mate said, 'Yeah, you couldn't be her. Michelle's got much bigger tits than you.' I soon changed my story, but then they wouldn't believe it was me. I suppose it was all good practice for being in the limelight.

After *Tucker's Luck*, I had a part in another drama for kids, in the Dramarama series – a lot of good stuff came out of that. I was in *Rip It Up* by Harry Duffin, a comedy set in a 1950s youth club (teddy boys and rock'n'roll versus ping-pong and hymn-singing – some choice!). Then I graduated to a grown-up play for Thames TV, *Miracles Take Longer* by John Kershaw. I played a desperate young mum whose baby has been taken by the council – heavy stuff for a sixteen-year-old. John himself was very encouraging, something I needed as I was making my way, getting experience. I remember he sent me a kind note – 'On today's performance you will be Dame Elaine quite soon!' I'm still waiting for the call to the Palace, though.

Then came a BBC Play for Today – remember those weekly plays? Prestige drama, taking on challenging issues. I played the title role in *The Amazing Miss Stella Estelle* by Leslie Stewart. Stella is a fourteen-year-old schoolgirl, who spends her evenings singing old Sixties hits in seedy working men's clubs, painted up and dancing about like a precocious doll. Jailbait, really. She's pushed into it by her greedy family, who need the money as no one else is working. It's a drama about exploitation – she's being robbed of her childhood, and not just by her family. Her audience is in on it, too.

I mention this play for a particular reason, apart from name-dropping Play for Today, of course – and yes, I was proud to be part of it. What got me was that people kept asking me if the play was a reflection of me and my family, just because I happened to have been a child performer myself. Crap! The publicity for the play mentioned it, and journalists brought it up in interviews. I just couldn't get it, so I found myself spelling it out that yes, I had performed on the West End stage in *Annie* at the age of twelve, but no, I had not been pushed into it by my parents. They were nothing like my screen parents. I was an actress because I wanted to be. What happened to any character I played was nothing to do with my real life. After all, I didn't have to be an orphan to play Pepper.

I was even interviewed by Selina Scott on *Breakfast Time*,

my first experience of the daytime sofa, and, frankly, felt as if I was being pushed into saying what people wanted to hear.

After a clip from the play, Selina explained to the audience that 'Stella Estelle's unemployed father and brother compete for her attention and her mother watches as the family disintegrates …' Then, after I talked about *Annie*, she asked me, 'Did *your* parents push you into going along to the auditions?'

No, I said. My parents were really pleased for me, but they were worried that I'd lag behind with my schoolwork, but it was all carefully supervised …

Selina pressed on. 'So the Stella Estelle we see there is not *absolutely* the same as you? Is there *anything* that resembles you in any way *whatsoever*?'

Me: No.

I was getting a bit uncomfortable now.

Selina asked about the other children in *Annie* – were they pushed into it by their parents?

Some might have been, but most of the children really enjoyed it.

Oh. 'So stardom doesn't weigh as heavily on young people as we thought it might?' asked Selina.

Not as such, no.

Oh well, thank you, and now for Nick and Glyn and a summer pudding …

Doing the Play for Today was the first time I'd come across that line of questioning, and I didn't like it. Still don't. I know it happens to actors all the time, getting identified with the parts they play – especially in soaps when they become so familiar to the audience. And often in soaps the scriptwriters do draw on something in the actor's own personality, as I was to find out years later. I suppose it's a handy hook to hang things on, but it can be taken too far.

*

I did go on to do other bits of TV, but mostly I was working on the stage – live acting again! I hadn't had that experience for years, since *Annie*. In 1984 I was in *It's My Party* by John Flanagan and Andrew McCulloch, at London's Greenwich Theatre. It was about a students' reunion that turns sour, and I played the daughter of one of the students. The next year I moved north, to the Royal Exchange in Manchester, playing in *Class K* by Trevor Peacock. This was a comedy-drama musical about anarchy in the classroom, with a bunch of society's rejects – who reminded me of one or two people I'd known at school ... I played the 'viper-tongued' Tina, spitting and snarling my way through the play.

Trevor sent me a letter that I treasured for years – I tend to hang on to such things. They cheer me up. He said, 'Dear Elaine, The moment you walked into that dreadful, tatty room for the audition – I knew you were going to be our Tina, but what I couldn't possibly have known then was how completely and richly you were going to fulfil the role.'

Come to think of it, was that a compliment?

Whatever, it was a lot of fun. By now I was feeling more confident on the stage, which was just as well as my next job was an even bigger challenge: working on *Animal Farm* for the National Theatre in Peter Hall's adaptation of George Orwell's classic fable. I played Minimus, the poetry-writing pig, and it's just about the strangest part I've ever played. I had to extend my range, darling! Actually, I wore a pig mask and waddled about on all fours with the help of crutches – pretty hard going.

What made the job even more exciting was that the company then went on tour with the play. We went to Vienna and Zurich, and then on to Canada, where we performed in Toronto, Baltimore and Vancouver. For me, who'd only gone abroad a couple of times to holiday hotspots in Europe, this was really travelling, and the tour seemed to play well.

It was while I was in Toronto that I met a man, an actor, who I was to be with for some years – my first long-term relationship. I was never one to racket from boy to boy. In fact, I was all of eighteen before I lost my virginity (good Catholic girl that I was). What I remember from that event makes me cringe with embarrassment, but not for the reason you'd probably expect. It wasn't that bad.

When I told my friend Michelle, she said, 'Oh, you must tell your mum. You're so close to her – she'd be devastated if she found out later and knew you hadn't confided in her.'

'What?' I said. 'Are you kidding? I'm not telling my mum.'

'Oh, you must,' said Michelle. 'It'll be another bond between you.'

Hmm ... I wasn't so sure. Still, Michelle seemed convinced. There might be something in it. So one day, when Mum was cooking in the kitchen, I said, 'Mum, just to let you know, I've lost my virginity.'

'What's that yer sayin'?'

'I've lost my virginity – I wanted you to know, cos we're so close and Michelle said cos we're so close I should tell you I've lost my virginity—' I was gabbling by now.

'Will ya stop goin' on about the virginity!' said my mum firmly. 'I was very close to my mother, but there are just some things you do not tell yer mother. And losin' yer virginity is one of them!'

So I crept out of the kitchen, crimson-faced.

It was a while after this that I met the bloke in Toronto. He'd stay with me when he was in London on business – I was still living at home in Matthews Court. Mum was always polite to him, but she didn't like him.

'No,' she said (out of his hearing), 'I don't like him. He's a vain man, thinks far too much of the way he looks. Any man who takes longer than a woman to get himself ready in the mornin' is no good at all!'

Mum was always a shrewd judge of character. What she really meant was that he was no good for me, and she was right. I was strong and resilient in other ways, but where men were concerned I was emotionally vulnerable. When you lack confidence, as I did, it makes you susceptible to a certain type of man, a man who wants to control you. This man was quite a bit older than me – thirty-eight to my nineteen – and though I didn't realize it at the time, he used to undermine me by playing mind games. A typical ploy was to say I was fat – and we all know what a terrible thing that is to be! I became borderline anorexic, sometimes eating just a handful of grapes a day, but fortunately I didn't tip over into full-blown anorexia. Something in me resisted that.

Why I kept with the man for so long, I'll never know, except that I've always been terrible at finishing things. It took me ages to get round to giving him the elbow. I wished I'd done it long before.

*

On the professional front, I had a few parts here and there on TV and on the stage, but around my mid-twenties, work started to tail off. I didn't know why – people had seemed to appreciate my work and I'd had some good reviews. Occupational hazard, I suppose. It's a risky profession, and hugely overcrowded. I'd been lucky to do as much as I had.

I started to wonder if it had anything to do with my accent. Being cockney had worked for me when I was younger, but perhaps producers didn't think I could speak any other way. I do have an ear for accents, though. Irish from my parents, of course, and Scots, and I'd learned an American drawl for *Annie* without too much trouble. True, talking posh didn't come naturally, and still doesn't – it just doesn't sit easily in my mouth – so perhaps I was never going to play middle class. At the time, there just weren't that many parts for female cockneys – this was before Albert

Square was on the scene and transformed it. Most of the roles would be as prostitutes or criminals – you're never seen as a proper grown-up with a proper job and a mortgage.

What to do, then? By now I'd moved out of Matthews Court into my own flat, on the ground floor of a Victorian conversion, with a wilderness of a back garden. It was only a short walk from my mum's, so I could still see her, though probably not as often as I should. I had to pay the rent somehow, so had to do something that would bring in the money, but still allow me the freedom to go for auditions if anything cropped up. I hadn't given up on acting by a long chalk.

I hit on the idea of being an aerobics instructor. By now, the late Eighties/early Nineties, the fitness craze had really taken off (never gone away, has it?). There were loads of celebrity workout videos like Jane Fonda's, and fitness studios were popping up all over the place. Play to your strengths, I thought – I'd always been athletic. And I did it all by the book, getting properly qualified at a place in the West End.

It wasn't well paid, but it covered the rent. And if I landed a part, then I could take time off. On TV I had parts in everything from *Dangerfield* and *The Bill* to *Casualty*, *Prime Suspect* and *Minder*.

Talking of *The Bill* reminds me of an occupational hazard for jobbing actors – going up for a part time and time again and always being turned down. I auditioned for that show more times than I can remember, for the kind of characters (working-class cockney) that I could do standing on my head, and every time it was, 'No, sorry. You didn't get it.' Why not? What was wrong with me? And if they turned me down every time, why did they keep asking me to try for something else?

I was seriously getting the hump – especially as the auditions were held in some godforsaken place out in the wilds of south London, in what looked like a desolate industrial estate. Took me hours to get there, and hours to get back. It just wasn't worth the effort, and I told my agent so. The show called me several more times but I just thought, you can stuff it. It really gets you down, erodes your confidence, when you keep trying for something and you don't get it, and there's no reason offered. You do begin to think, maybe I just can't hack it. Then the show called me again, and my agent pleaded with me to go up for it – 'Just one more time' – and kept going on till I said, 'Oh soddit, all right.' So, not in the best of moods, I traipsed out to the industrial estate, and wouldn't you know it, this time got the part. A heroin-addicted prostitute – there's a surprise. Still no call for a cockney barrister, then.

Still, it was a job, and I couldn't afford to turn it down. And anyway that would be my stint in *The Bill* for the foreseeable future. TV series always allow some time to elapse before using an actor in a different role, otherwise there's a chance that viewers might recognize the face and get confused. You don't want anyone thinking, 'Hello, I've seen that barrister before. Wasn't she a heroin-addicted prostitute a while back?'

So, picking up the odd bit part on TV, but wanting more than anything to be a full-time actress again, I persevered with the aerobics. Until I got put off by a gym in Highbury that I worked in. I know they have to make money, but this gym was just too pushy for me. When people tried out the gym, I was supposed to really twist their arm so they would buy membership, on which I'd get commission. The woman running the place really believed in giving it a hard sell, but I just couldn't do it. Some of the people dropping in were obviously hard up. Why try and persuade them to join the gym, I thought, when they could go to a leisure centre – or just run round the park?

This attitude did not go down well. I moved on, picking up part-time fitness work, hoping for news from my agent. I did get a bit part in a British film, the crime thriller *Face*, which was great, but there was nothing much else on the horizon.

*

By now, I wasn't living alone in my flat. I'd started my second long-term relationship, with another actor. We did have something going for us for a while, but it was dead long before we actually split. Again, I was shrinking from ending it. But when I did, as far I was concerned, it was for the best possible reason …

Meanwhile, I'd been working in London's fringe theatre, a long way from the Victoria Palace! Tiny places, usually above smoky old pubs, with a fantastic buzz. I loved the rawness, the immediacy, the whole excitement of something new and different. I appeared in a couple of plays by Mick Mahoney in the Old Red Lion, in north London. I played Sugar, a prostitute, in his play *Shift*, a stunning urban love story packed with his trademark sharp wit and energy. Then I was Lorraine, the sister of two gangsters, in *Fantasy Bonds*, his hard-hitting drama of criminal power games.

I also worked at the Bush Theatre, in *Boom Bang-a-Bang*, by Jonathan Harvey, who managed to make a sell-out comedy about people gathering to watch the Eurovision Song Contest. Takes some doing. This was directed by my old mate Kathy Burke, who'd been branching out for quite a while by now, doing more and more directing.

She was back to acting, though, when I next worked with her – we were both in the film *This Year's Love* (well, her more than me). Then I played her sister in *Gimme Gimme Gimme*, the mad TV flat-share sitcom where she's the grotesque man-hungry slapper Lynda La Hughes and James Dreyfus is the camp would-be actor Tom. Jonathan Harvey's the writer – he'd seen me in his play *Boom-Bang-a Bang* at the Bush, and thought I'd be right for the sister, Sugar Walls (another Sugar, and another pro, of sorts). Wonder how many viewers realized what the name meant – bearing in mind Sugar's sex-mad exploits, think about it ... Totally outrageous stuff. I don't know how Kathy does it – heavy-weight drama one minute (like her Queen Mary Tudor in the film of *Elizabeth*), crazy camp comedy the next, never afraid to try anything – and never letting her accent stand in her way either. She's more than lived up to the potential she showed at Anna Scher's – phenomenal talent. Now I can hear her saying, 'Shut up, you twat' – so ...

The couple of episodes of *Gimme, Gimme, Gimme* I was in were certainly the high point of my year. Everything else was pretty dreary – money running out and a big tax bill looming, no calls from my agent, not exactly sweetness and light on the home front. Not that any of it really mattered, though, compared to what had been happening to my mum.

One day in 1999, my lovely, vibrant mum took an overdose of pills. It wasn't enough to kill her, thank God, so it was probably what everyone calls 'a cry for help', but nobody had realized she needed it. Sophie and I were shocked rigid. We hadn't seen it coming at all. Were we blind? Too wrapped up in our own lives and our own problems? Or had Mum, with typical unselfishness, put on an act and disguised how she was feeling until she couldn't bear it any longer?

By this time, Mum and Dad weren't living together. Their relationship had continued to be tumultuous – I'll talk more about this later – and Dad had finally left some years back. On the surface at least, Mum had been her usual self, keeping the flat in Matthews Court immaculate, working the hours she wanted – she was always in demand for bar work – keeping company with her many friends and, what's more, finding a new love, a wonderful man called Doug. He was relaxed and very good-humoured, he really looked after her – he took her on some great holidays – and they enjoyed a close, loving relationship. They still kept their separate homes, though (Doug lived out in Epping), and it was an arrangement that evidently suited them both down to the ground.

When any of us tried to talk to Mum about her overdose, she'd make light of it – 'Just a silly mistake' – but of course we were all worried.

Months went by, and Mum seemed to be OK. She hadn't needed any medication at all, and we began to relax. I just pushed the worry to the back of my mind and got on with life. We celebrated the new millennium and hoped that things would only get better …

They did. I finally had some good news from my agent, and when I told Mum she was thrilled for me and seemed like her old bubbly self. So I could relax and enjoy it too. I did tell everybody else – it's hard to keep it to yourself when you're asked to audition for *EastEnders*.

In fact, I'd been called to audition before, but it was a good job I didn't get the part. Bizarrely, the character was quite posh, not one of the locals, so why I, with my particular accent, was called, I have no idea. When I was next called, the part would be right up my street (or rather Square). It couldn't have come at a better time – I was skint, and nothing else was on the horizon. Last Chance Saloon time.

*

The way auditions were held was changing. The traditional way is for an actor to read from a prepared script, playing the part of a character created by the writer. That was what I'd been used to as a professional actress. And soaps were no different – just like any other kind of drama, writers would work up their characters' backgrounds and present the actors with a ready-made biography and personality. Funnily enough, though, the way I auditioned for *EastEnders* this time took me right back to Anna Scher's approach, as it was all about improv.

The show had a new executive producer, John Yorke, who'd been an *EastEnders* script editor for years. With writer Tony Jordan, he introduced the idea of actors' workshops, where people could improvise all kinds of scenes, mixing and matching, chopping and changing. The idea was that new characters would grow out of the actors' own personalities and experience – not carbon copies by a long chalk, but based on something real, something viewers could believe in. It makes a lot of sense, especially when you think that soap actors may be appearing in up to four episodes a week – they're practically living their characters. Much better all round to go with the flow. After all, like the best soaps, *EastEnders* is essentially about real people living in the real world, even if some of the plot lines are a little OTT, and it needs to have an authentic feel. This way, the storylines grow out of the characters, rather than the other way around.

By now the show had been running for fifteen years, since 1985. It hadn't taken long to become a national institution, giving *Corrie* a run for its money – and a chance of employment to a lot of actors with cockney accents!

Anyway, as my agent told me, there were no specific parts up for grabs – John Yorke and Tony Jordan were planning a major new storyline, which would involve introducing a whole new family to the Square, and they just wanted to see people who might fit in. This was a bold move. It can be tricky enough introducing a single character into a long-running soap – when viewers have got used to the cast and don't like change – let alone a whole family. I was to learn later why John Yorke had included me in those invited to audition. It turned out he'd seen me years before in Mick Mahoney's *Fantasy Bonds* and had thought I was 'brilliant'. I believe him (still had to do the bloody audition, though!).

The day after my agent had rung me, I went to the studios at Elstree. I met up with a load of other hopefuls, and we were sorted into various groups. We were off.

First I was put with another woman and a man, and we went through our paces with different scenarios. I think the producers were a bit naughty – at one point they said that the other woman and I were to be lesbians. Now I really wanted the job, but if I had to start snogging a complete stranger I'd be a bit uneasy if she went for it too much. In the end we played it straight, so to speak, and just chatted in character – I copied my gay friends, who don't go around snogging all over the place, larging it. Then the bloke had to come up and try to chat us up, not knowing we were gay. Very dramatic!

The other woman, Tonia Kerrins, was brilliant, and I could tell right away what a good actress she was. A lovely, special person too. I remember thinking that even if I didn't get a part, I'd made a great friend in Tonny. I was right. Some years later she'd be my baby's godmother.

In one of the breaks between improvs, I got chatting to the bloke in our group, talking about parts in *EastEnders*. I told him, 'Don't be a doctor; they never get a proper part.' One of the writers heard me and laughed. I thought, I'm in here …

We acted out a couple more scenarios, including one with the man asking me out and me being all shy, then it was a case of 'piss off, go home and wait. If you haven't heard from us by six o'clock this evening, then forget it. If you hear from us before then, you're back tomorrow morning.'

I got the call. I was back there next morning, and so was Tonny. Fantastic! We'd both got over the first hurdle – but this was just the start of a long, long process. We were all tested with different scenarios, in different combinations of actors, who were gradually whittled and whittled down to a core group – all women. By now, it was becoming clear that the new *EastEnders* family would be dominated by women – often the case in soaps, isn't it?

Tonny and I always thought that only one of us would make it. 'It's gonna be you,' we'd say to each other. 'No, it's gonna be you,' would come the reply. Or perhaps neither of us – the other girls up for parts had blue eyes, and both Tonny and I have brown …

Tonny made it to the very final hurdle, then she was lobbed off. A mistake, in my opinion, as she's a bloody marvellous actress. She was devastated, having put so much effort into everything. Mind you, later on, when she saw what happened to me, she wasn't so sorry to be out of it.

By now the new family had a name – Slater – which brought back some unwelcome memories of that toerag who'd hurt me twenty years ago. Laila Morse would be the grandmother, Mo, while Jessie Wallace, Kacey Ainsworth and me were the sisters – Kat, Little Mo and Lynne. After nearly three months we'd developed a real chemistry between us – it was almost as if we were real sisters and had grown up together. At one point we even did a turn as the Nolan Sisters, which apparently went down well.

Things were getting more intense now, more demanding. We were given bits of scripts to act out, we went along to the set and did bits to camera. The writers were sent videos of us so they knew how the characters were shaping up, what they looked like and what they sounded like. The four of us still hadn't been formally told we were in, but it began to look more and more likely.

The fourth sister, Zoe, and the dad, Charlie, hadn't been involved in the earlier auditions and were only introduced in the final stages. So was Garry Hobbs, who would become my character's husband. Laila, Jessie, Kacey and me duly went through our paces with several different Zoes, Charlies and Garrys.

It was one Thursday that we finally got confirmation – we were in! The Slater family had been created and would burst, fully formed, on to TV screens within a few months. All that preparatory work done by Laila, Kacey, Jessie and me had welded us into quite a formidable unit, and we felt really strong in our characters – and what a mixed bunch they were.

Laila had worked Mo (or Big Mo, to distinguish her from her granddaughter Little Mo) into a tough matriarch, who's been widowed for twenty years. She's hard as nails, but will do anything to protect her family, including petty crime, like fencing dodgy meat. Jessie's Kat was the glam one, a good-time party girl who loves to flirt and go clubbing, but at heart is loyal to her family. Kacey's Little Mo couldn't be more different from her gran – she's a mousy little thing, afraid to raise her voice, a bit of a doormat, but happy to help anybody, and she's very domesticated. Her sisters take the mick out of her, but they're protective of her at the same time. She's married to Trevor, played by Alex Ferns, a nasty piece of work who's often violent towards her. My Lynne was the eldest sister, down-to-earth and hard-working, generous, but a bit gullible. She was jilted at the altar once and is terrified of ending up on the shelf. All she really wants is to settle down, get married and have kids, preferably with her laddish boyfriend Garry, played by Ricky Groves – though he's got a roving eye that keeps getting fixed on Kat.

To complete the family, there's Zoe, the youngest sister, played by Michelle Ryan. Nearly seventeen, she's beautiful and can't wait to grow up, which will get her into all sorts of trouble. The dad, Charlie, played by Derek Martin, is a decent bloke who works as a cabbie and looks out for his daughters.

The family's back story had been carefully worked out too. They'd moved to Albert Square for a new start, after Charlie's wife Viv (Big Mo's daughter) died. There's a link already, in that Big Mo's husband Jimmy was the brother of Pat Evans (Pam St Clement), who was already well established in the Square. Not a friendly link, though – there's been bad blood between them for over thirty years, ever since Pat told Jimmy that Mo was having an affair (she wasn't).

So there we were – a mini soap opera in ourselves, ready to move into 23 Albert Square, a house converted from some flats. It happened to be where a character, Reg Cox, was found dead in the very first scene of the very first episode of *EastEnders* – we hoped it wasn't an omen …

*

I'm not gonna be poor any more! That was my first thought when I knew I'd got the part – so much for artistic sensitivities. But that tax bill had been weighing heavily.

As the news sunk in, I was absolutely 100 per cent thrilled. All I wanted to do was act, I was desperate to act, and now I had my dream job. I'd be working in a long-running show, one where I could use my natural accent. *EastEnders* is like gold for cockney actors. I'd feel right at home, and for the icing on the cake I'd be joining old mates like Todd Carty, and other actors who'd gone to Anna Scher's. I'd just missed Gillian Taylforth, who was in the group above me at Anna's – I've known her all this time.

She's adorable, and I was sorry we weren't going to overlap – be a bit difficult, though, as she had the job in the café that my character was due to take over. Funnily enough, we've both got deep voices – geezers' voices, we call them. Wonder if it was a requirement for the job?

I celebrated in style, with a very select party at my place, including Kathy, of course, and Tilly Vosburgh – a big thank you to everyone who'd been so supportive while things were rocky. Kathy and Tilly, who'd had so much success, warned me that my life was about to change. There'd been a note of caution, too, from John Yorke and Tony Jordan when they'd told us the good news. 'Your lives will never be the same,' they warned us. 'The press will be on to you, and watch out if they get their hooks into you.'

Yeah, yeah, I thought, never in my life having been actively pursued by the tabloid press, I can deal with them.

At least it started well …

CHAPTER FIVE

Soap and Scandal

Exterior scene – a street.

'Scuse me,' I say to a passer-by, 'we're lookin' for ... what was it again?'

'Yer dozy moo,' says my silver-tongued boyfriend Garry, 'Albert Square.'

With that riveting exchange, the newest *EastEnders* arrive in style – well, in a white van – me and Garry and sister Kat in the front seat, with the rest of the family following on.

So the Slaters took up residence in the Square, among all the other families whose antics had kept the nation enthralled for years – the Fowlers, the Mitchells, the Wicks, the Watts, the Butchers ... We'd soon add our own quota of emotional traumas, family skeletons and edge-of-the-seat suspense.

Not that we were an immediate smash, it must be said. Some viewers thought there were just too many of us, and that our arrival upset the balance in the Square. Others thought we were too loud and lairy – us? Never! But it always takes time for new characters to settle in and become part of the scenery, and in fact it wasn't long before the audience got the hang of us, what we were all about, and began to warm to us.

The press certainly had a field day. We were front-page news all over the place, especially us four sisters. (The truth about Zoe wouldn't be broken for quite a while. If you don't know what that is, and mean to watch the show on DVD one day, look away now. She's really Kat's daughter – our uncle raped Kat when she was only thirteen. No lack of drama in our family!) There were endless features setting the scene of our arrival, giving our back stories, endless speculation about how we'd all fit in, or not as the case may be. Headlines like 'THEY MAKE THE SQUARE SIZZLE' and 'FOUR GORGEOUS GIRLS MOVE IN' – thanks for that.

The things we did for publicity ... In one shoot we were called 'Charlie's Angels' (Charlie being our dad – geddit?), where Jessie, Kacey, Michelle and I were all dressed in dramatic black and struck suitably angelic poses – or perhaps we were pretending to hold guns, I'm not sure. I liked the title of another spread – 'Soap Dishes', where we were given gorgeous frocks to wear and talked about our beauty routines. I never thought anybody would ever care about mine (and yes, I do have one). But of course it's all part of the game and goes with the territory.

We first appeared in the September of 2000, and it wasn't long before the Christmas bulldozer kicked in. For one paper the burning question was what we'd wear for Christmas and what kind of parties we liked. So I was honest and said something like, 'Chilling out with mates, having a drink and a good laugh.' Bearing in mind later developments, I might just as well have worn a T-shirt with 'I'm a pisshead – remember that' on it. I also mentioned that I'd be spending Christmas with my mum and whatever I wore would need an elasticated waist as my mum's Irish and likes to feed the five thousand. Funnily enough, my appetite for food has rarely featured in any publicity …

I found all the attention a bit overwhelming, to tell the truth, as I just wasn't used to it. I'd learned Anna Scher's lessons very well – that fame wasn't the point of acting, it was the experience itself that mattered. That probably makes me sound like a poncy twat, but that really had been the way I'd approached acting. I was learning that working in a soap isn't like other kinds of drama. Because it's ongoing, in the nation's living rooms so many times a week, your profile is bound to get raised. The sheer fact that you've worked hard to make your character believable means that millions of viewers do believe in you (well, most of them realize you're not real, but you do become literally a familiar face). And where there's public interest, there's press interest. Which comes first, I've often wondered. Do the papers break a story because they know their readers will like it, or do they break a story and whip up the interest? Both, probably.

With the large cast that a soap has, there's bound to be a steady supply of people behaving badly, one way or another, at least by tabloid standards, and *EastEnders* was easy pickings from the start. I think the first splash was raking up the past of Leslie Grantham (Dirty Den, landlord of the Queen Vic) – years before, he'd been convicted of murder and sent to prison. That was a juicy bone for hacks to get their teeth into. After that, they had to make do with sex and drugs and booze, one at a time or all at once.

The press interest in all long-running soaps seems insatiable, as I was soon to learn, and even when you leave the connection stays with you.

*

Those first three months were a whirlwind. Glitzy press coverage aside, us new arrivals had a lot to get our heads round. It had been drilled into us that the most important thing of all was the Schedule. It's a complicated business getting three episodes out each week – and four from 2001. Everything has to be meticulously planned, so that every member of the cast and crew is in the right place at the right time to do the right job. The actors are only the visible bit in the end product. Behind them is an army of production people – producers and directors, along with their assistants, script supervisors and runners, plus a whole load of people working on the technical side – cameras, sound and lighting, design, scenery, costumes and make-up. Everything for everyone must be planned down to the last dotted i and crossed t. Any one thing going wrong, or any one person getting out of line, can seriously screw things up.

As an actor, you're on a rota with anything up to fifty others, a rota that has been very carefully worked out. You have to accept that often your time isn't your own. If your first scene is to be shot at eight in the morning, then you have to be at the studio at least an hour earlier, to go through make-up and costume. Even if a soap character looks unmade-up, with plain old clothes, it takes work to get her like that! And if your next scene isn't until late at night and it's outside in the Square, where the scenes are shot in natural light – well, you just have to wait.

And of course you have to learn your lines in good time. In the old days, when the show went out just twice a week, I think the actors had the luxury of a whole day or two to rehearse, but, with more weekly episodes, the work rate was cranked up and rehearsal time reduced to the minimum – then straight into the scene. If you're in a big storyline, the pressure can get heavy. Usually it's a Monday-to-Friday job, but you'd have to do a Saturday, too, if time was especially tight. And there was no going off to the Seychelles when you felt like it – you had to fit in your holiday allowance around your storyline, too, though there is time off over Christmas.

Another thing to learn was how to get round Elstree. When I first went to the studios I was a bit disappointed. I wasn't expecting Hollywood glamour, but it looked more like a factory site, all boring warehouses and office blocks. Of course it's more interesting once you go through the gate and get on to the actual lots where the show is filmed.

Albert Square looks so real! Well, of course it does, it's supposed to. Set designers and builders work miracles – you'd never guess those solid brick-built houses and the pub are just façades. The ground is real, with solid roads and pavements, and the greenery in the garden is real too. Filming in the open air here has its drawbacks, though. It's usually about six weeks before transmission, so there's a time lag. You could be dressed in a skimpy top for summer when it's actually bloody freezing. And wrapped up warm on a boiling hot day.

Interior scenes are all set up separately on big stages. That's where you walk into very realistic-looking living rooms, bedrooms – and the Queen Vic, of course. You have to find your way through this maze, learning which is which and where it is, and how it relates to the exteriors, so you can orientate yourself at all times. It tickled me to find out that in actual fact the interior of the pub couldn't physically fit inside its exterior shell, but that's all just part of the illusion, isn't it? (Though I gathered that some viewers get their tape measures out and write in, pointing out this anomaly …).

In those early days, us newcomers were also busy getting to know the existing characters, both personally and on the set. And they of course were getting to know us. For some of the older hands, it must have been unsettling to have so much new blood arrive on the show all at once, but everyone soon adjusted. Wendy Richard and June Brown were especially kind and welcoming, along with the living legend that is Barbara Windsor, who must surely have achieved the status of National Treasure by now.

I was only the latest in a long line of Anna Scher students. As I said, I'd just missed Gillian Taylforth – Patsy Palmer and Susan Tully had also left by now. Sid Owen, who played

Rickie Butcher, and Gary Beadle, who would arrive a year after me to play charming rogue Paul Trueman, were also Anna Scher boys. Great blokes both.

And I was happy to see other old mates when I arrived – ex-Tucker Todd Carty (playing Mark Fowler) and Perry Fenwick (Billy Mitchell). I vaguely knew Steve McFadden (hard nut Phil Mitchell), through our mutual friend, the brilliant playwright Mick Mahoney. I was to find that Steve is a lovely man, who proved a true friend to me, a tower of strength. I can't speak too highly of him. He's a generous actor, too – I've always thought it was a shame that our respective storylines didn't cross much. I'd love to have acted more with him.

*

It was a good job I'd had all those years of acting experience behind me. I had to learn particular things for *EastEnders*, of course, and adjust to a very demanding schedule, but I never had any trouble learning lines. What began to get me down was the waiting around – I'd had a taste of that working on feature films, but on *EastEnders* the time between scenes seemed to stretch interminably. I began to wish a twelve-hour working day really did mean twelve hours' work, and not one hour either end of the day – at least I'd be busy.

Still, why should I complain? We actors were getting very well paid, and it was hardly gruelling in the circumstances. I was acting, and I loved it. The only problem was how to fill all that spare time. I'm a great reader, so that was one good way. But I'd eventually get tired of sitting by myself in my dressing room, and gravitate towards the bar, which was nearly always open. I say 'bar', but it was more like a social club, with food laid on, and snooker tables. What with everyone's overlapping schedules, it could get very busy, especially around lunchtimes, and you could always be sure of someone to chat to. As well as the good company, of course, there was the drink ...

Yes, it's Lordan the Lush. Drunk as a Lordan. And so on. After my honeymoon period with the press, that was my popular image. (Not popular with me, you understand.) In the following year I was to have many a news article devoted to my drunken antics. Now I've never pretended I don't like a drink. I come from a hard-drinking Irish background, where booze was always on tap. Though that doesn't mean that we all had to be alcoholics. My dad liked a drink, but he was rarely the worse for it, and it was very unusual for my mum to overdo it. The drinking wasn't the be-all and end-all, it was the lubrication for the party. Of course some people we knew did succumb, like my lovely Uncle Jerry, Mum's brother. What made it worse was that he worked in a pub, so temptation was always at hand. He got more and more damaged by the drink till he eventually had a massive heart attack that killed him far too young.

Myself, I'd hang out with friends, knock back too much vodka and sometimes make an exhibition of myself. Nobody took any notice until my face started to be familiar on the box, then I – just like other people in the public eye – became newsworthy.

Two things get me about this – well, more than two, but these for starters.

One, I was a grown-up woman – I might not always behave like one, but I wasn't hurting anybody else. Just doing what thousands of women do all over the country. I'm not saying it's a good thing, I'm saying it's not unusual, I'm not a freak.

Two, I was criticized for being a drunk by journalists, who didn't even know me! What's more, are hacks known for clean living and sobriety? My arse. The all-out bloody hypocrisy of it.

What's more, once they think they have a handle on you, you get actively pursued, hounded. Then it's not just coming out of nightclubs, which I suppose is fair game. It's when you have paparazzi hovering about near your home, waiting for you to emerge in the morning not looking your best, so of course the caption can get in a dig about hangovers. And they twist facts to suit their own agenda. So if I put wine bottles in a bin down the road, that's because I'm hiding the evidence of my wild binges. While in fact I just didn't want to fill up my own bin with bulky rubbish – I'd put newspapers in the public bin too. (In case the eco lobby gets on my back, this was before the days of recycling bins – I now recycle everything that is recyclable, OK?) And of course, if I popped to the local shop, I wasn't buying a bottle of milk, it would have to be booze.

You might be thinking I'm going on too much. A highly paid actress, don't know she's born, stop complaining – if you don't like it, get off the box? That's the tricky thing. If people make accusations and you ignore them (sticks and stones ...), they're not afraid to up the ante. On more than one occasion I've been told that the press had a field day with me because I wouldn't take them to court. Mind you, litigation is a risky business, and can backfire even if you have a justifiable case. It's also horrendously expensive. If, on the other hand, you do stand up and issue a statement, it looks like they've got to you and their poison has worked, then there's more publicity and plenty of column inches saying you protest too much ...

You can't win. I suppose what I tried to do was just get on with life, enjoy my fabulous new job, spend some unaccustomed money, have a good social life and not worry too much about everything else.

But then something happened that put all that stuff into perspective, reminding me what really matters. My sister Sophie had been rushed to hospital and was fighting for her life.

*

The roots of my sister's illness in 2001 had begun ten years earlier, when she became clinically depressed. It was the first time a member of my family had suffered from depression – this was before my mum showed something was wrong by taking an overdose in 1999. I tried to understand, to help, but found it all very mysterious. I'm told you can't really appreciate what depression is like unless you've suffered from it yourself, and I guess I'm one of the lucky ones. The lows I've experienced have had all too obvious causes.

But Mum and I knew she was in distress. A young woman who seemed to have everything going for her – her own flat, a good job, an active social life – and seemed happy, began to behave strangely. Obsessively. Something had happened in her psyche to put her into hyperdrive. She just couldn't function normally.

So of course Mum and I turned to the doctors. Sophie was sent to Friern Barnet Hospital in north London. Mum and I drove her there. It was a huge, elaborate Victorian pile, and if ever a place was designed to lower your spirits, it's that one. It used to be called Colney Hatch, when it was an old-fashioned lunatic asylum. Of course it had been modernized by now, but the corridors were still grim and endless – I remember them as more like tunnels, radiating all over the place like a labyrinth. Grey walls, grey floors, grey, grey, grey – and the disturbing noise of screaming and crying ... Mum and I were filled with dread, but we were assured that this was the place that could help Sophie. So we left her there, thinking, right, they'll make her better. We didn't know any different.

I was still living with Mum at Matthews Court at the time, and drove us both home. We were crying our hearts out, leaving Sophie in that place. As I slowed the car to a stop at the bottom of the road, my mum suddenly started laughing uncontrollably. I thought it was the upset getting to her, but 'Look at him!' she gasped, pointing out of the window.

It had been raining, and there was a huge puddle in the road. In this puddle was a big shaggy dog, attacking his own reflection. He was growling and barking and scrabbling with his claws, furiously fighting himself. He got angrier and angrier, jumping about. It was so funny – Mum and I just howled with laughter, clung to each other, our eyes were streaming. Talk about comedy and tragedy. We were in a highly emotional state, I suppose, and the dog just set us off. Not that we knew it then, of course, but tears of sorrow were more in order for Sophie.

In the hospital, it seemed they just pumped her full of drugs, which kept her quiet. They proved to be highly addictive, and she's never been off them since. With hindsight – and knowing more about mental illness – Mum and I would never have gone along with her treatment. With great strength, Sophie has managed to put her life back together, but that experience left its mark, and it was her record of mental illness that would be used against her when a physical illness threatened her life years later.

Sophie had already been diagnosed with gallstones, and was waiting for the operation to remove them at the local hospital. So when she developed severe abdominal pains, she went to Casualty at the same hospital. There was a long queue and she was left unexamined. The pain grew worse, she was in agony. She begged for attention, but was brushed aside, told to wait. She couldn't stand it – she kicked up a fuss and at one point vomited. Whereupon two big security guards threw her out, for causing a disturbance. When my mum phoned and complained, she was told that somebody had looked up her records and seen that she'd been hospitalized with depression. So of course that had to mean she was making it up, just attention-seeking. This is the label you get when you're mentally ill.

Next day her agony was worse, so my mum called the doctor, but he was a locum, and just prescribed antacids. The following day, a Thursday, Sophie was in so much pain that she was throwing hot water on to her abdomen in a hopeless attempt to relieve it. Right, thought Mum, I'm not having this.

She phoned for an ambulance, knowing that Sophie would have to be fast-tracked through the system. Sure enough, when she got to hospital she was rapidly diagnosed. She had pancreatitis, a life-threatening condition – and one that is a known risk factor for people with gallstones. And this is the same hospital, remember, that made the diagnosis of gallstones in the first place. They should have been even more alert to her condition.

The system swung into action at last, and Sophie was taken to intensive care. Mum and I went to see her as soon as she was settled. That first time, she had a little oxygen mask over her mouth and nose. The next day she had a bigger mask on her face. On the third day she was swamped by a huge one. Next day, at eight o'clock in the morning, Mum got a phone call from the hospital. They were terribly sorry, but Sophie's lungs had started to fail and they'd had to ventilate her. They'd had to smash her front teeth to get a vent down her as she couldn't breathe on her own.

Sophie was in a coma. The doctors thought she was going to die. She had the last rites several times, performed by our local priest, Father Joe.

By this time, Mum and Dad had been living apart for years. In fact Dad was living in Stevenage with his new partner, Eileen. He himself had been diagnosed with a serious illness a couple of years earlier, an illness with no hope of a cure. It's called progressive supranuclear palsy (PSP) – the same condition Dudley Moore suffered from. It affects the brain, like Parkinson's. But Dad was still mobile, and Eileen drove him down to see Sophie every day. He'd sit by her bed, looking at his daughter being kept alive by machines pumping in and out, his daughter who couldn't know that he was there. Mum was there every day, too, and I came as often as work allowed. We were willing her to live. At the same time my heart would be breaking for my dad, who was bravely coping with his own increasing infirmity.

Yes, I was still going to work. But then I was told that I had to go to Brighton, for location filming. I said I'd go, but only on condition that if my sister got worse – and it was touch and go – I'd be out of there right away. To be fair to *EastEnders*, they agreed absolutely. There are times when life is more important than rotas.

Sophie did come out of the coma, thank God, after a

long four months. She was left with a damaged foot, which makes her limp. We were all just so happy and relieved to get her back.

I tell you this story as it says so much about the attitude towards mental health, even today, in the twenty-first century. The previous year I'd seen my old friend and mentor, Anna Scher, slide into depression. Later she would be stigmatized, thought to be unfit to run her own theatre. Sophie too was stigmatized – it was as if, with her history of mental illness, she couldn't be telling the truth, she had to be fabricating her physical illness. Not only is this unjust, it's dangerous. And a few years later, the system would fail my mum, too – and this time the result would be utterly devastating.

Meanwhile, I duly went off to Brighton for the *EastEnders* special shoot. Sophie was on my mind of course, and Mum knew where to get hold of me. I was just hoping that concentrating on work would make the time pass quickly.

What I didn't anticipate was meeting the love of my life.

*

What the tabloids really, really like is when they see parallels between an actor's screen life and their real life. That was what I resented all those years ago, with *The Amazing Miss Stella Estelle* on TV. I didn't realize at the time that it was such small beer! What with soap news getting as much prominence in tabloids as real-life news, it's a double whammy for them if they can combine fact and fiction. One feeds off the other. Sometimes the real name and the character's name are interchangeable. And people seem to lap it up.

Not that my love life attracted much attention when I first joined *EastEnders.* I was still living with my long-term boyfriend in my Highbury flat, and by then our relationship was nothing to write home about. We were just drifting, but neither of us would take the initiative to end it.

While my character in *EastEnders* was being set up for a complicated, long-drawn-out love triangle, which was to last well into the following year, I wasn't looking for love myself, certainly while I was preoccupied with Sophie. And I didn't immediately recognize love when I found it.

I wouldn't have seen Pete Manuel much before now, even though I'd been in the show for about six months. As the studio resource manager, he was always busy making sure that the right technical crew were in the right place at the right time, and he'd have been working primarily in the gallery. It's called a gallery, by the way, as years ago it really was up high, looking down on the studio floor. Now it's also down on the ground, and is actually the control area. There were three of them on *EastEnders*, one looking after the sound, one looking after the lighting, and one – Pete's speciality – looking after production. He'd be in there with the director, the vision mixer and script supervisor, while us actors went through our paces on the studio floor.

Whatever it was called, there'd be no galleries on location …

Cast and crew were put up in a hotel, and one day after work we were all relaxing in the bar. I was drinking with some of the crew members and looking at a book we'd come across, a history of the hotel. There was a cartoon in it that made me laugh, a woman with a huge fat arse. The crew were laughing too, and as this man I didn't know drifted by I drew his attention to it.

My first impression was that he was very rude. 'That's not funny,' he said firmly. A kind thing to say, but not what I wanted to hear. All I could think of to say back was, 'Well, you're not funny either.' Whereupon I bought the whole crew a drink, but left him out.

I obviously hadn't put him off, though. Perhaps he saw me as a challenge. One of the production people was throwing a birthday party that night and we all went. Pete and I got chatting, and this time there was a real connection. I found him warm, funny and incredibly attractive. Not conventionally handsome – handsome can be boring, I've found. I like what goes on in the heart and the soul. He seemed to be attracted to me ... By the time we went back to London, we were inseparable.

Pete didn't hide the fact that he was married. Of course, he'd have to be married, what's more with three young children. Just my luck. When I did know, it was already too late. I was committed, but all too aware of the implications.

Let me say here that I was not looking for a married man. When I was fifteen and thinking about my future life, I didn't say to myself, 'Right. I'll go for a married man – even better, a married man with children. That'll make for an easy life. I could really do with all that baggage.' But you can't choose who you fall in love with, and if that sounds corny – tough. It's true.

I had to ask Pete when it was that he first fancied me – after all, I'd have been visible to him on the studio floor for months.

'*Tucker's Luck*,' he said promptly.

Apparently he'd fancied the pants off me all that time. Mind you, as Michelle, Tucker's girlfriend, I was carrying some puppy fat at the time. Pete's always been on the large side himself, so he probably thought he'd be in with a chance there. I call him my fat George Clooney lookalike, which you probably don't need to know!

After the shoot, we returned to our respective homes. Back working in the studio, I don't think our affair was secret for long. When you're so much in love, it's hard not to show it. He would be eating lunch at one table in the canteen, and I'd be at another, but we couldn't help gazing at each other. Or he'd make excuses to come on to the studio floor. And the temptation of suddenly disappearing into my dressing room! I remember one time when Pete was due back in the gallery, and dear June Brown was chatting to someone outside my room. Pete could hardly sidle out unnoticed, so I went out and asked June if I could have a word, taking her by the arm, encouraging her down the corridor and probably talking bullshit. I don't know what she must have thought, but it gave Pete a chance to disappear.

We felt the same about each other, and about our dilemma. Exhilarated at being in love, but fearful at the same time. There was the inevitable prospect of Pete telling his wife, and me telling my boyfriend. Though as I say, my previous relationship didn't have much going for it, for either of us. Pete had by far the more painful prospect. His children, two girls and a boy, were the most important consideration for him.

When I visited Sophie in hospital, while she was in a coma, I used to tell her all about Pete, even though she couldn't hear me. I was hyper, desperately worried about my sister but giddy with emotion. I'd never known what it was to be in love like this. No wonder they write so many songs about it!

I think it was then that I started to earn my reputation as a drinker. It's so easy, when you're wound up, to reach for a bottle and smooth away the rough edges in your mind. Blot out the anxiety, the guilt – yes, I did feel guilt that I was seeing a married man. I'd never set out to hurt anyone. Not that I'd ever need an excuse for a drink, to be honest. As I say, I've always liked it, liked the taste, liked the effect. But as my poor Uncle Jerry had found out the hard way, everyone thinks they can hold their drink, and most don't realize when it's getting hold of them. When it becomes a necessity, a prop-you-up rather than a pick-you-up. Friends and family might get anxious, but you brush off their concern. She's a lush – I'm a happy drinker, I'll have you know.

I could never hide anything from my mum. She noticed a change in me, and her suspicions were aroused. So I told her.

'I'm in love,' I said.

'Indeed?' she said. 'Who with?'

'He's a married man,' I said.

Small explosion.

'A married man with three children,' I added.

Bigger explosion.

'What! Have I got two feckin' daughters to be worryin' about now?' my mum demanded. 'A married man! With three children! Now you just finish with him!'

'OK,' I said.

A couple of days later she said to me, 'Have you finished with the married man yet?'

'Yeah,' I said. 'I'm not seeing him any more.'

'You'd better not be!' my mum shot at me.

A few days later she collared me again. 'Are you lyin' to me?' she demanded.

I had to admit the truth – how much in love I was with this wonderful man I'd met at work, and I had no intention of ever giving him up.

'Are you mad?' my mum burst out. 'He's just bloody usin' you, can yer not see it?'

She was only just warming up. 'I'll give him feckin' work! I'm comin' down to Elstree and I'm gonna stand by the gate, an' when I see him I'm gonna kick his bloody bollocks in!'

Not one to mince her words, my mum.

*

Spring turned to summer, and at last Sophie was out of danger. We brought her home from the hospital, and she started her convalescence.

That was one huge weight off the mind, but Pete and I had still not come clean about our affair. We were wildly happy when we were together, but it was painful to be apart. We knew that we'd have to face things eventually, but we kept putting it off and putting it off, squeezing in just a bit more time together and delaying the inevitable. By then I was really hitting the bottle.

In early July, my affair with Pete and the drinking collided. Disaster. I was at Elstree, staying the night in my dressing room as I'd had a few too many drinks and didn't want to risk driving. Ironic, as it happens. Pete was fine, and had driven off home. Then I got a call from him – he'd had an accident, crashed his car, he was hurt, and could I come and pick him up? Could I! Any idea about not drinking and driving flew right out of my mind. Usually I'd never be so stupid, but I was so anxious about Pete. He could be really hurt.

I jumped into my Audi and zoomed off to where Pete had said he was, on a grass verge near the A1 Barnet bypass. It was getting on for midnight when I found him, and apart from a bloody nose he was OK, thank God. His car was a write-off, though, and I went cold as I thought how bad it could have been. He'd had a lucky escape.

It was then that we made a mistake, a huge mistake. We tried a cover-up. If we went through the usual formalities – accident report, police, insurance and so on – it would be bound to come out that we were together. And while, as I say, it wasn't so much of a problem for me to tell my boyfriend, for Pete to tell his wife and break up his family was going to be shattering. We just weren't ready.

We started to panic. I had awful heartburn and was shaking. Perhaps we should pretend we'd both been in my Audi, we thought, so we started moving stuff from Pete's car to mine. That's when some policemen spotted us and came up to investigate.

We made up a story at first. Pete said the crashed car wasn't his, and I said no, I hadn't been drinking. The cops soon proved we were lying – Pete had the keys to the car in his pocket, and I failed the breathalyser. A right Bonnie and Clyde we were.

What a nightmare. The police took me in their car to the station in Borehamwood, while Pete drove there in my Audi. Normally he could have accompanied me, but there was no room – I was squashed in the back seat beside a stack of bloody traffic cones and other paraphernalia.

After the usual booking procedures, which included a cheek swab for DNA, I was put in a cell. Apart from the time me and Debbie were put in a cell, after our escapade in Piccadilly, this was the first time for me, ever. It was awful. I felt like absolute shit – unlike the last time, I didn't feel like singing.

Pete was allowed to join me in the cell, and we were eventually let out in the early hours of the morning. A truly horrible experience, which I deserved. There's no excuse – I blew it. A danger to myself and others. I should have thought more clearly, got a friend to drive – oh, I don't know. I just rushed to my Pete.

I had a call from the *EastEnders* press office saying the *News of the World* had heard I'd been arrested for drink driving, and was it true? God, the paper was quick off the mark – I was about to tell the office myself what had happened. At least there was no mention of Pete yet.

The case went to court, but dragged on with adjournments on technical grounds. Each time I was in court, it was a peepshow for the papers again, who rehashed the whole thing.

Another thing that made the headlines that summer were reports of my cavortings in a nightclub, with Jessie Wallace. We'd had a great time, fans had bought us drinks, and as we came out the door we tried a bit of a cancan, kicking our legs up and in my case revealing a bit of arse cheek. Well, that's civilization gone to the dogs. That picture is now a fixture, dragged up again and again to point the finger at either of us at any given opportunity.

It was two or three months later that shit began to hit the proverbial fan – about my drinking, I mean. My affair with Pete still seemed to be off the radar to the wider world. It was also when I realized the *EastEnders* press office wasn't going to be my best friend.

One Friday evening a press officer called me at home and said, 'We've had a report that you were drunk and ran through a plane telling everyone it was going to be hijacked. Did you? And that you were arrested when you got off the plane at the airport. Were you?'

What? It's true that I'd just flown back from Spain. Pete had been working there on an *EastEnders* special and I'd secretly joined him. I told the press officer that I'd been drinking – I usually have to have a couple on a plane to settle my nerves – but that I certainly hadn't run through the plane shouting ridiculous things. And no way was I arrested, though I did remember something that puzzled me at the time. As I got off the plane, another passenger said to me, 'You're gonna be in trouble when you get to work next week.' I didn't know what they meant at the time, and frankly I didn't care.

Now I asked the *EastEnders* press officer, 'What shall I do?'

The answer? 'Get out of your house.'

Well, that was what the press office was there for, to look out for the interests of *EastEnders* people in the media. They must know what they're doing. So I quickly packed a bag and went round to Kathy Burke's place. Next morning, people were phoning me to say there was a pack of press outside my door, reporters and photographers. I had to stay away for days, and holed up at Tilly Vosburgh's for a while, too.

Looking back, I should have stayed put and come out to

confront them the next morning, so I could set the record straight. Just as I'd suspected, it was the person who'd spoken to me on the plane who'd fed this particular bit of fiction to the paper, but another national paper had checked the story with the airline, who had refuted it. The airline said that if anybody had done what I was accused of, they most definitely would have been arrested, especially after 9/11.

I begged the press office to allow me to tell my side of the story by going on *GMTV* or something. But they insisted on 'No comment' – and of course the accusation stuck, and has been regularly recycled in the press ever since.

It began to dawn on me that I was being treated rather differently from other people on the show. Here she goes, you might think, making out she's being got at. But it did seem to be the objective truth that when other people on the show got in a mess, either they were allowed go on TV and put their side, or else the matter was airbrushed out.

As for my affair with Pete, it must have been common knowledge in the studio by now, but still there hadn't been a sniff of it in the press. Work was usually a hotbed of gossip, and it wasn't unknown for somebody to grass when something was going on. Pete and I were expecting someone to spill the beans on us – in fact we half-hoped they would. Then everything would be forced out into the open. I admit we were being cowardly, but we really didn't want to hurt other people. We should have come clean, but we hung about, making the most of each moment, putting off the day when it all went pear-shaped. And that day wouldn't be far off.

We realized our affair was all round the studio when John Yorke, the executive producer, called me into his office. Now, I've nothing but respect for John, and I know he meant well.

'Listen,' he said, 'you've got to sort yourselves out. You know if the press get hold of this they'll blow it all up, and things'll get messy. So decide what you want to do. If you want to stay together, then stay together, but sort things out.'

He was right about the 'messy'.

*

What made our affair irresistibly juicy for the tabloids was the way it overlapped with my character's story. It just so happened that Lynne Slater had desperately been trying to get boyfriend Garry up the aisle, but he'd always let her down. True to form, he failed to turn up for the wedding rehearsal, and she wasn't best pleased, so when womanizing Beppe di Marco started circling round, and reckoned he fancied her after all, things got really complicated.

From then on it's will she won't she, will he won't he – the wedding's on and off … and on again, at which point Beppe sweeps like the US cavalry into the register office and tells Lynne not to marry Garry. All high drama that kept the ratings up!

There was one light moment for me in all of this when, as the soap bride-to-be, I did a publicity photo shoot modelling a selection of wedding dresses. Gorgeous stuff – white, ivory, scarlet and gold. I was duly asked what I'd wear if I got married in real life, and I remember saying something like,

'I'd personally have a small wedding – a quiet affair with a few friends and family, something very low-key.' Well, fast forward a few years and I wasn't far wrong!

Before Pete and I could get married, though, there was a whole lot of shit to get through.

He broke the news to his wife at the end of November. It was as painful all round as can be imagined.

A week or so later, we made front page tabloid headlines – EASTENDERS STAR SEX SCANDAL – you'd think that nothing else was going on the world, but that's the tabloids for you. The story was full of the predictable stuff about stealing another woman's husband and being a real-life home-wrecker ... and guess what Pete was? A 'love rat', naturally. Oh, and 'sizzling sex sessions', of course – when did they ever do anything but sizzle?

Apparently I'd been going round bragging all over the shop about our 'steamy romps' (when the sessions weren't sizzling enough, I suppose) – that's when I wasn't too drunk to stand. There was even a snap of me shopping in an underwear department. Just looking for knickers? Oh no – 'sexy lingerie'.

The press started stalking both our homes, so Pete and I holed up for a while at a friend's flat in Hertfordshire, near the studios. Before the story broke, Pete had gone up to Yorkshire, where his mum and sister live, to explain things to them in person – he didn't want them finding out through the papers. When he came back, I asked him how his mum had reacted to the news.

'Well,' he said, 'my sister had forewarned her a bit, so when I told her the whole story she wasn't that surprised. Not over the moon, she said, but in a way she'd seen it coming.' Then he said that whatever his mum thought, she was never one to interfere, she just always looked out for him and would support him as far as she could.

His mum, Millie, demonstrated her support in a subtle way just as the story broke. Pete got a call from his wife. She'd phoned his mother, to tell her that there'd be stuff in the paper next morning about her son that she should watch out for. Pete was full of concern, and immediately phoned Millie himself. She told him that she'd replied, 'Listen, lovey, as I said to her, with my cataracts I wouldn't be able to read it anyway!'

What a wonderful woman! She's very close to Pete and his sister. Their dad died when Pete was only fifteen months old, from diabetes complications (the kind of thing that can be controlled these days), so Millie brought up her two children virtually single-handed. Times were hard, but Millie got through them with true grit and a great sense of humour. I always know when Pete's on the phone to his mum, even if I'm out of the room, because there's so much laughing and cackling. She gave her children a great start in life. I didn't meet her face to face for a while, but we talked a lot on the phone. One of the things she said to me, in her distinctive northern accent, was, 'Now, lovey, now you two have found each other, you stop smoking!'

Back in Hertfordshire, Pete and I stayed in our friend's

flat until Christmas, when Pete went back up north to stay with his mum and I went to my mum's. Meanwhile, the *EastEnders* office tried to defuse the publicity by announcing that I would be given a three-month break from work to sort out my 'personal problems'. In the new year, Pete came to live with me in my Highbury flat – the old boyfriend had made himself scarce. I wouldn't introduce Pete to Mum yet, knowing how she felt about the whole affair. Then matters were taken out of my hands.

Pete and I had a row, some silly nonsense (lovers don't have the odd row? Then they're not lovers), and he popped down to the local pub. My mum happened to be in there, with her partner Doug, and it was Doug who recognized Pete from his picture in the papers. He pointed him out to my mum: 'Look, Bernie, the love rat!'

Mum went over to him, all brazen, and said, 'Hello there.' Pete took one look at her – the dark, sparkling eyes, the glam get-up – and immediately knew who she was. 'You're Elaine's mum, aren't you?' he said.

'I am,' said Mum, 'but where's me daughter?'

Pete was sheepish. 'Well, to be honest, we've had a bit of a row and I've come here for a quick pint. Can I buy you a drink?'

Mum looked him up and down. After a moment, she said, 'Yes, you may.'

Pete bought drinks for all three of them and they sat down at a table together. He was smoking a small cigar, so out of politeness he offered one to Bernie and Doug.

Bernie took one – 'Yes I will, thank you very much' – and proceeded to smoke it. This gesture was obviously out of politeness too, as she told Pete later that she'd never smoked a cigar in her life. She managed to carry it off, though.

Meanwhile, Pete phoned me up on his mobile. 'I'm in the pub with somebody,' he said. 'Guess who?'

Somehow I knew straight away. 'My God,' I said, 'you're with my mum and Doug, aren't you? Will you bring them both back here?'

So Mum and Doug came back with Pete, chatting like old friends. 'Well now,' she said to me, 'well now. I've met yer feller. And he's all right. He has a lovely head of hair!'

No, that's not a euphemism. Pete's hair is indeed thick, while mine has always been fine and flyaway, a disappointment to my mum, whose own hair was thick and glossy. She must have been thinking of our future children and their lovely heads of hair.

Later, she told me – and this will always stay in my heart – that she fell in love with him immediately, and she could tell how happy we were together. For the rest of her life she and Pete were the best of friends.

*

As part of me being sorted out, the *EastEnders* office arranged therapy for me with a properly qualified therapist. He must have been qualified as he charged 120 quid an hour. I was going to talk about my guilt at having an affair with a married man, that's why I was drinking, blah blah blah.

The first time I walked into the therapist's office, in a big posh building that looked more like a hotel than a hospital, I was struck by the number of family portraits all over the place – pictures of him, his wife and kids were everywhere. I wondered whether this was supposed to signify anything – work with me and you too can play happy families?

Anyway, I talked to him about what had been going on – my 'issues', I suppose you'd call them. I told him about the press and how upset I was with what they wrote about me. The next time we met, he greeted me with, 'Have there been any more stinkies about you in the press?' – which became my little gag. Every time I went I used to play a game, see how many 'stinkies' I could work into the session. I'd walk in and say, 'There's been a couple of stinkies this week!' And I used to bet with my regular cab driver – this place was miles away, and he'd pick me up every time and take me back. I'd say to him, 'Right, how many stinkies do you think I'll get in this time?'

He'd say, 'Go for twenty.'

'No,' I'd say, 'thirty. If it's thirty I get a free ride home.' (Not really, of course, I always paid.)

Then I'd come out and say, 'Thirty-five! Stinky, stinky, stinkies everywhere!'

You'll have gathered that therapy wasn't for me. I know it works for some people, but not for me. I'm sure *EastEnders* arranged it with the best will in the world, but if anyone was going to get my life back on track, it'd be me. With a little help from my friends, of course. I'd certainly need it, with all the stinkies that lay ahead …

CHAPTER SIX

Bursting Bubbles

Well, the shit had well and truly hit the fan, and was getting splattered all over my life. But the worst was over, I thought – me and Pete are out in the open, no need to sneak off and tell lies. It'd be painful, especially for him, but we'd work things out.

Just as I got back to *EastEnders*, there was a nicely timed interview with Pete's wife splashed all over one of the tabloids. She saw me as a 'predatory cat' with no morals, pursuing her husband ruthlessly, wrecking the happy home … and it was all doomed anyway because my biggest love was alcohol. Well, of course. Who wouldn't be hugely angry and bitter? Nothing I could say would make any difference. Except that Pete's a man of the world and can make his own decisions. I'm not a hypnotist.

Shortly after that there was another tabloid story about me being a drunken slag, getting banned from a hotel and generally being a pain in the arse. This occurred shortly after my on-screen wedding, so I was described as something like 'newly-wed café girl'. It was the usual dilemma – do I reply or not? I chose a dignified silence, only adding the information that on the night in question, Pete and I were alone together and far too busy to get involved in anything else.

Despite the bravado, the stories slagging me off do hurt and I can't say they don't, even while I try to rationalize them. I sometimes wonder whether tabloid readers ever think of the person behind the image, the real human being behind the headlines. Perhaps they don't. Perhaps they think anyone with a bit of fame is fair game. I'm not talking about mainstream showbiz gossip. It's the calculated cruelty that gets me, especially with women's appearance. Photographers going out of their way to snap a patch of cellulite, a spare tyre bulging over a waistband, a bad hair day – what do readers really get out of it?

My mum had been keeping a big scrapbook about me – it started when I was younger, with my reviews for TV plays and the stage. Then there were the happy shiny early days of *EastEnders*, but by now my publicity was very different. 'I'm callin' this book *The Good, The Bad and the Ugly*,' Mum announced. 'Will you look at it, you've more front pages than Britney.' Not exactly true, it just felt like it.

There were more headlines later that year, when my drink-driving charge came to court. More rehashing of my drink-sozzled lifestyle and – as my *EastEnders* character was being Torn Between Two Loves – my affair with a married man. My solicitor was pleading a technicality, and the case was adjourned. In retrospect I wish I'd pleaded guilty, but it dragged on to the next year. And again people would believe what was reported at the time – that I'd actually said to one of the policemen, 'Don't you know who I am?' As if! I've never said that, not even as a joke. But it's stuck.

*

Meanwhile, and more importantly, I was trying to build a relationship with Pete's children. I didn't meet them for some months – Pete would go over to them by himself every fortnight and take them to the pictures or swimming, just making sure he was there for them. Then during the summer they started to visit us in Highbury now and then, staying over in the flat. I so hoped that we would get on, that they wouldn't blame me, and see me as a wicked stepmother – and in the event things have worked out better than I dared hope. I won't embarrass the children by going on about how wonderful they are – but they are. They're a real credit to their mum and dad. No way am I trying to take their mum's place – they call me Elaine, and I feel more like a big sister to the older daughter, who's thirteen. Pete remains, of course, the best dad in the world.

One time the children were due to stay with us, and the *EastEnders* office informed me that I'd have to turn up to work that weekend. It was coming up to Children in Need, and the cast were performing a special in Albert Square, a short piece that included 'Singing in the Rain'. I'd planned to be with Pete, who wasn't working on the special, and the children, so I told the office I couldn't make it.

'I can't do it because Pete's children are coming,' I said. I didn't want to miss seeing them and it was important for us all to spend time together.

'But the script's written,' they said.

After a bit of arm-twisting, I said, 'Oh, all right, I'll do it, but only if I can bring the children on to the set.'

There was some grumbling, but when Pete told them that he'd be with the children, and of course he knew the protocol on set, and he'd take care of them, it was agreed.

The children had had a trip to the set before, but this time it was special. They had a great time. Steve McFadden was especially kind to them – he's great with kids, being a family man himself. In fact *EastEnders* did a really nice thing, including the children as supporting artists – never say 'extras' – in an interior scene, in the café. The girls were thrilled to be part of it, while their brother was far more interested in what was going on in the gallery or helping the cameramen – like father, like son.

Well, that was a rare moment of harmony for me and the show.

*

If ever I felt singled out for special treatment by *EastEnders* – and that's not 'special' in a good way – then it was the time a Phil Mitchell storyline took the show to Portugal. Pete, of course, would be going with the crew, and as I wasn't due to film any episodes, I thought I'd go out there and stay with him for a few days.

'You can't,' I was told. 'It's a closed set.'

What? Not only was I a member of the regular cast, but Pete was my partner – we were openly living together now – and other partners of cast and crew members were going out.

'What d'you think I'm gonna do?' I asked. 'Hang about the set and wave like a fan?'

But no dice. They were adamant. In fact it got quite iffy – so many other people going out, and not me. As I say, it wasn't as if I was needed in Elstree for filming – that would have been a perfect excuse for them to refuse to let me go. But I wasn't needed at the time, I wasn't asking for any scenes to be rescheduled, all I wanted was to go out and be with my man. What were they scared of? Apparently they thought my presence would attract the wrong kind of attention from the press.

Pete told me that when he got to the location more than one cast member asked when I'd be coming out – they'd taken it for granted that I'd be joining him. Taken all round, this did feel very unfair, with other cast and crew members' family and friends being allowed to go out.

Then there was the time that I'd booked a day off so I could go to my friend Tilly Vosburgh's wedding. This was a really big day, one of my oldest and dearest friends getting married, so I took the precaution of booking it three months in advance. As bad luck would have it, on the day before the wedding there was a torrential downpour that flooded the studios at Elstree. We could film in the open, in

Albert Square, even when it was raining quite hard, but this time it was like hosepipes – hopeless. We were all gathered together in the bar area and told that schedules would have to be changed.

I was booked for one scene. 'I hope you're not thinking of scheduling my scene for tomorrow,' I said. 'I booked the day off three months ago.' After all, it wasn't for just any old day out, but a once-in-a-lifetime occasion.

But no, I had to turn up and film some stupid stuff about buying a wooden pigeon or something. I know the schedule is important, but my piddling little scene could easily have been rescheduled. So I missed Tilly's wedding. I made it to the do in the evening, but I would have loved to be there at the ceremony. And when you know that arrangements can be made for other people – have been made for them – it starts to rankle.

I'd really begun to feel unsupported, unappreciated, on *EastEnders.* I don't mean I expected people to say, 'Darling, you were wonderful!' all the time – if ever – but the odd 'Thanks' or 'That went well' wouldn't have gone amiss. Hearing other people being praised for doing no more than I'd done made things even worse. I felt I was being pushed aside and marginalized – at the same time reminding myself that I'm a professional and should rise above it all.

Most of all it would have been nice to have had the chance to refute the stories about me in the press, or go on a chat show, like my fellow actors did, to prove I wasn't a total pisshead and could carry on an intelligent conversation. As it was, I was built up in the media to be something I'm not, and the only advice I got from work was ignore it, ignore it.

Was I getting things out of proportion? Looking back, I can see how that could happen. That's the trouble with mindsets. Once you've got one, once you've convinced yourself that this is the truth of something, it's difficult to get out of it. Whatever happens only seems to prove you're right. This way for paranoia …

There I was, priding myself on my professionalism – I always turned up on time to the studios, unless the traffic was awful, and I only overslept once when my alarm didn't go off. On the other hand, at times I did drink too much at work. It was too easy, during those long waits between takes … but no, no excuses. I drank because I liked it, I was bored, I was stressed by the horrible things said about me in the press. There was even the odd occasion when I'd had one too many while waiting to go on set, and I found it difficult to concentrate on my lines. That is embarrassing and totally unforgivable – you hold everyone up. I've no excuse for that.

So I must have been making the producers nervous – I can appreciate that now. Whatever my grievances, I was part of a complex, tightly organized operation where one person screwing up has repercussions throughout the system. I can't deny that, and it's something I really regret. All I can say is that, at the time, I was feeling genuinely stressed. I thought that once Pete and I were out in the open, things would settle down, but as well as my hassles with the press and work, his divorce was grinding through very slowly. Things were going to have to come to a head – and they did. At work, anyway.

*

One morning I felt a strange tingling in the palms of my hands and the soles of my feet. They'd come out in a bright red rash, the skin was peeling and the tingling turned to burning, like hot coals. I'd never had anything like it before, but realized it was most likely brought on by stress. I didn't go to the doctor, but managed to drive to work. Then the pain, especially in my feet, got worse, and I asked the office if they could supply a car for me until my feet were better. No, was the answer.

So I wasn't in the best frame of mind for one of our cast meetings – they're held regularly to discuss all sorts of stuff. To add fuel to the fire, I'd also had a couple in the bar.

The meeting was going on and on, and then one of the producers was spouting some stuff about how much he cares for us all. Cares? That was it for me. I can't listen to this, I thought, and before I knew it I was on my feet – my burning feet – saying, 'Whaddya mean, care? Look at my hands! D'you wanna see my feet? Don't tell me you care!' For good measure, I added, 'This meeting is overrunning. You're always going on about how we have to be on set on time, but we're gonna be late. You wouldn't be happy if any of the crew were late back. I've had enough of this meeting, I'm going back on set!'

With that, I stormed out of the room. As I went, I saw Gary Beadle making a throat-cutting gesture. Too right. I'd cut my own throat and burned my own boats. I had a valid point to make, but it wasn't the cleverest way of putting it.

They let me stew. I finished my scenes.

Then Louise Berridge called me into her office. A lovely lady – she'd replaced John Yorke as executive producer. I knew what was coming, though for a while I couldn't get my head round what Louise was saying.

'Can you give me something? Can you give me something so that I can keep you?'

Eh? Give her something? What did she want? A promise to sign the pledge or something?

The bottom line for me was that I'd had enough. Enough of feeling sidelined, unappreciated. It's been a great job, I've enjoyed myself enormously and made some great new friends, but I can't stand anybody saying they care when they so obviously don't. Or words to that effect.

It was the parting of the ways. I'd say I'd had enough, Louise would say that my character was being written out in order to make way for other storylines and the tabloids would say I was being fired for being a drunk.

Just my notice to work out, then – I'd film my final scenes in late spring or early summer 2004. As it happened, just to complicate things, I spent much of that time on crutches. I managed to bash my ankle while moving furniture at home, trapping it between a heavy bench and a table. I woke up next morning and it was really sore, I couldn't put any pressure on it. I took a lot of painkillers, and Pete drove me to work – he had to carry me to the car.

By the time I got to work, my ankle really hurt and the whole leg was looking more and more deformed, so I was sent in a car to Watford General Hospital. At this stage I was thinking it must be a bad sprain, or heavy bruising.

I was X-rayed, and then a lovely nurse came up and said, 'There's good news and there's bad news.'

I said I'll start with the bad – get it over with.

'Your ankle is badly broken,' she told me, 'and you'll need an operation.'

An operation! I'd never had an operation in my life. I'd never even been in hospital except to visit people. I was petrified. Quick – what's the good news?

'Your other leg is fine!' she said.

I tried to laugh, but I was crying. I phoned Pete and he was shocked, said he'd come straight away. Meanwhile, the doctors tried to manipulate the joint. They wrapped my leg in bandages and I was given gas and air, which I really took to, I must say. Halfway through this procedure, Pete hurried in and saw me being given the gas and air.

'Bet you didn't think she was having a baby!' the same nice nurse cracked.

No, I'm having an operation, one that would involve

inserting a bloody great iron bar up my leg. As complex fractures go, this was pretty complicated.

I had to let work know what was happening, so I phoned one of the producers and told her, 'My ankle's broken and I've got to have an operation.'

'Oh, right,' she said. 'Can you come back and just finish the scenes you were meant to do today?'

Hello?

I said, 'I'm gonna repeat it to you: broken ankle, operation. So no, I won't be coming back today.'

It was awful. I wouldn't be able to put any weight on that foot for over three months. I hopped around on crutches, and discovered a new use for Pete's computer chair, one with half a dozen little wheels. I could scoot all over the flat sitting on that, and give my arms a rest. I recommend it. By now, Pete had laid wooden floors throughout the flat, which made a smooth surface for the wheels. In fact he's brilliant at DIY and had transformed our little flat into something altogether lighter, brighter and more stylish. When I'd fallen in love with him, I'd had no idea he was so talented in other areas!

When I was out of hospital, I asked work if they could supply me with a car to get me to work and back. There was no question of waiting out all those weeks, and by now Pete couldn't give me a lift as he was working back at Television Centre in White City. They said I could have a car for two weeks.

'Do you mean fourteen days' worth of work, or just over those two weeks?' I asked.

I wasn't surprised to hear it meant just two weeks. At this time, it meant just three days of filming – they'd worked in the story that I'd slipped on the floor – so I was driven up and down for those three days. Very kind.

After that, my old friend Julie helped me – Julie who could never play out after school because her dad was so strict. By now she'd had three kids (she started young), and while she'd moved out of Highbury to east London, we still saw a lot of each other as her youngest child goes to Drayton Park primary school (following in a fine tradition), and her mum, who she's very close to, still lives in Highbury Hill. What a rock Julie has always been (here I'll do my Ali G impression and call her ma Joolie) – we've had great times together, and she's helped me through thick and thin.

Now Julie was helping me on filming days. She'd drive me in, and help me get into costume. So what if other people who'd had accidents were given cars and their own dressers, even though they were quite capable of bearing their weight with their injury? At least things were consistent.

The wardrobe people were lovely, but always pushed for time, so we were all grateful for Julie's help. That didn't stop management getting Julie thrown off the premises – she was practically frogmarched out. What for? Confidentiality. She might blab to the press – as if! Julie would never do anything underhand. She was eventually allowed to sit in my dressing room with the door shut. I moved awkwardly and found showering difficult. Someone had kindly put a white plastic chair in my shower, so I could sit down, and Julie heroically helped me in and out of the cubicle – she saw the eye of the tiger more times than was necessary for good friends, know what I mean? She also helped me at home – more than once I couldn't get out of the bath, and Pete was late back from work. One call on the mobile and Julie would appear like a guardian angel.

Meanwhile, my character was being written out and I was getting to grips with her new storyline. Poor old Lynne is not going to go out on a high. After being torn between cheating husband Garry and lover Beppe, not to mention old lover Jason – the one who'd jilted her at the altar – Lynne is allowed a brief period of happiness when she becomes pregnant, only to lose the baby when a fairground ride collapses on her in the Square. What's more, she's unable to have any more children, so she leaves her old disappointing life behind and goes off to pastures new.

After my final scene was shot, there was a little ceremony and I was presented with flowers, champagne and a present. I was genuinely touched. Then I made a brief speech, from the heart:

'I've met a lot of wankers over the years on this job and a lot of really gorgeous people. The wankers – bugger off. The good people – see you again.'

*

By now, I was even happier and more relieved that I was leaving *EastEnders*. I talked about having a new life, and not just my own … When the writers worked out my final storyline, they couldn't have known that I too was going to become pregnant. I found out just days before my final scene. And for once I welcomed life imitating art!

CHAPTER SEVEN

Our Little Fighter

The first time I had any inkling of that new life was a Saturday morning in May. I was showering as usual, and as I looked in the mirror, I thought, what's happened to my waist? It wasn't dipping in and out any more – in fact, it was decidedly straight. Then I thought, ooh, am I pregnant?

It's not like we hadn't been trying ... but not so long ago Pete had had a snip reversal. After three kids in his first marriage, he'd had a vasectomy, but by now we were totally committed to each other, and very much wanted a child together. A brilliant clinic had done the deed, and he's got a DVD to prove it! Yes, really. Not the sort of thing you show with your holiday snaps – it's actually a record of the operation, made as the surgeon did the op.

Only one way to be certain – I sent Pete up the road to get a pregnancy test. Sure enough, there was the little line saying positive. But don't get excited yet, we thought, better make sure. So off Pete went up the road again to get another test, a different type. Another positive – no doubt about it: I really was pregnant! We were thrilled (and Pete thanked the surgeon).

I soon got myself sorted. Off to the GP, where I said I wanted to go to the Whittington Hospital. It's where I was born, so I thought it would be a nice touch. Everything seemed fine for the first two or three months, then it wasn't. Pete and I couldn't know at the time just how bad it would get.

*

First there was a spina bifida scare, after a blood test showed something wasn't right. 'Have you been taking folic acid?' the doctors asked me, and as I had they thought that was very unlikely. But still, they said, to be on the safe side I was to have a detailed scan. Before taking it, I had to drink lots and lots of water until my bladder was full to bursting, as this makes the images clearer – you just have to keep your legs crossed and hope you don't have to walk very far.

As it happened, the scan showed up a light patch on the baby's lung, and the following week I was sent to a special unit at UCLH – London's University College Hospital – for an even more detailed scan. I was under the care of Professor Charles Rodeck throughout my pregnancy. He and his team are absolutely fantastic – he's a man who inspires great confidence in all his patients, and he kept in touch with me even after the baby was born.

Looking back now, I can see that as Pete and I first went through the doors of the hospital, it was the start of a new way of life for us, one in which the hospital would become a kind of second home.

After the first scan, we were taken to a side room – never a good sign, I think. Doctors aren't going to break bad news in public, are they? While the doctors were discussing the scan among themselves, my mind was racing. What was wrong with my baby? Was it Down's syndrome? I was in my late thirties, after all. If it was Down's, children can still have a good quality of life, can't they? I sat gripping Pete's hand, unable to put my fears into words.

The doctors duly delivered their verdict. 'It isn't spina bifida,' they said, 'but what we call a c-cam – a lesion on the lung.' This sounded scary, but they said it wasn't cancer. Its proper name is cystic adenomatoid mass of the chest – a serious condition, no getting away from it, but there are well-established ways of treating it, so the baby had a good chance. I'd have to be closely monitored with regular scans every other week.

Every time I had a scan, all the medical people were very friendly and encouraging. To make us feel better, to get things in proportion, perhaps, they'd say things like, 'Yes, the c-cam is serious, but at least it's not a diaphragmatic hernia – now that can be very dangerous.' I gathered that's a condition when the baby's abdominal organs – stomach, liver, bowels, and so on – grow through the diaphragm into the chest cavity, squashing the heart and lungs. So I'd lie there thinking, right, things could be worse.

And they were.

When I was six or seven months pregnant, Pete and I were ushered once more into that little side room, our hearts sinking. Wish this room wasn't painted blue. Not exactly cheerful.

Can't be good news, we thought. It wasn't.

'The diagnosis has changed,' the doctor said, and kindly and sympathetically, he told us that in fact the baby did have a diaphragmatic hernia, which had allowed the bowel to grow through into the chest cavity. I'd have to be even more closely monitored for the rest of my pregnancy, with scans every week towards the end of it.

Again the doctor was encouraging – there was talk of surgery, the very latest techniques, the best possible care … I'm not sure that Pete and I took in all the details – we just sat there rigidly, trying to contain the shock, to keep our breathing steady. Why was this happening? Did I do something wrong? What causes the condition?

We were assured that it was nothing to do with what I had or hadn't done – the cause isn't known exactly, though genetics may play a part. That didn't help us. We'd never even heard of the condition, and in fact it's very rare. In the shock of the diagnosis, we both had the same unspoken thought: would our baby even be born alive?

I don't know how we got through the next weeks. There was none of the usual happy anticipation of a baby's birth. We knew our baby would be staying in hospital, so there was no rush to buy nappies or a cot or clothes, though nothing could stop Pete's mum knitting! Still, I'd look at stuff in Mothercare …

What made things even worse was that the tabloids were

still sniffing around. The last episodes I'd filmed for *EastEnders* wouldn't be going out until early July, so I suppose I was still newsworthy. Around the time I discovered I was pregnant, I was pictured celebrating Arsenal's Premiership win – yes, in a pub. I was supposed to have been involved in a drunken brawl with some strange woman. My recollection is that I was picking up broken glass from the ground as there were little kids around, and someone had wanted to beat up Lynne Slater from the telly. What can I say?

There was a worse intrusion later on. Someone actually phoned my GP's surgery and pretended to be me, asking for blood and urine test results! Can you believe it? Fortunately, the doctor's receptionist knew me very well and realized it wasn't my voice. After that, we had to agree on a code word to make sure nobody on the staff gave anything away to the wrong person.

That might have stopped one kind of intrusion, but of course there were others. Tabloid hacks always know how to put the boot in. On my way to the hospital, or even popping out for a loaf of bread, they'd snatch photos of me – hardly looking my best, but why the hell should I? I was pregnant, tired and eaten up with anxiety about the health of my baby. So there'd be the FRUMP WITH A BUMP headlines over a picture of me looking dowdy and frazzled. I tried not to let it get to me.

There was one incident, though, that was the worst ever. I was just walking to the local shop when a car cruised alongside me. There were two men in it, one with a camera. 'Hey,' he yelled through the open window, 'lift yer head up!' I kept my head down, shielding my face, and hurried along the pavement. The car kept pace with me, and the man screamed out again. 'Lift yer head, yer fuckin' cunt!'

That was too much. My legs gave way and I sank to the ground, arms over my head, crying. It was just like being bullied at school all those years ago, but by bigger, meaner bullies.

I don't know what they would have done if another car hadn't come along. The driver, a man, got out and yelled at them. 'Hey, leave her alone, you fuckers! You can see she's pregnant – get the hell out of here.'

The first car drove off, with more shouting and cursing, and the man helped me to my feet. I was so touched by this concern from a complete stranger that I started crying all over again. But it's good to get a reminder that there's decent people in the world, when you see so much of the scum.

*

I kept attending hospital every week, until early December. I was about thirty-five weeks now, and after what turned out to be my last scan, on a Thursday, Pete and I were taken yet again to that small blue room.

We braced ourselves. The doctor said, 'We don't want to wait much longer. The bowel obstruction is getting worse, putting a lot of pressure on the baby's lungs. We want you to come in on Sunday, for a caesarean section the next morning.'

Thank God for that, I thought – thirty-five weeks isn't that premature, and the sooner he's out, the sooner he can be made better. (By this time we knew our baby was a boy.) Meanwhile, I was to take steroids, to help his lung development – and, with Pete, get a taste of what was to come.

The doctors had told us that as soon as he was born, our baby would be ventilated – helped to breathe by a machine. Of course, everyone's seen that sort of thing on TV, and I'd visited an intensive care unit when my sister Sophie had been on life support, so I thought I'd know something about it. Pete had never been near one in his life. We were advised to go to Great Ormond Street, the world-renowned children's hospital, where our baby would be taken for surgery soon after he was born. In the intensive care unit there, we would have a chance to see how sick newborn babies were treated, so we'd be prepared.

Prepared? What I'd seen before didn't prepare me for this – and it was entirely new to Pete. As a lovely lady showed us round the unit, and we saw those tiny, doll-like babies, with tubes and wires coming out of them, we broke down – cried our hearts out. We were really, really upset. At the sight of those frail little bodies, fighting to stay alive – and at the thought that our own newborn baby would have go through it all himself ...

In fact, though, it did prepare us. If you'd said to me at the time that we'd get used to ventilators and the whole medical paraphernalia, that we'd end up taking everything in our stride, I'd have laughed in your face – or cried. It just goes to show that you don't know what you're capable of until you're put to the test.

But I'm getting ahead of myself. On the morning of Monday, the 13th of December 2004, our son was born. He was to be called James, after both his grandfathers – my dad may have called himself Garrett, but that was actually his middle name. One of the nurses kindly told me that as the birth was a high-risk procedure, it would be a good idea for James to be photographed as soon as he was born … a tactful way of saying that this photo might be our only memento of him.

So there I was in theatre (theatre! Why isn't there another name for something so absolutely removed from enjoying yourself on stage?). Surrounded by lots of medical people, lying on the bed, a green curtain across my chest, screening off the business end. I don't care what they say about too posh to push – the caesarean was wonderful! The epidural had something to do with it, of course. Pete was by my side, all keyed up, holding a camera to take the first picture – only it turned out not to be the one we'd wanted …

As soon as James was brought out, he was taken to another part of the room to be ventilated. Pete went over to get a good shot of him, but in the scrum he was jostled and turned round the wrong way. He clicked the camera just as it was pointed at me – with my whole belly opened up. That's one photo that won't go in the album – it's almost on a par with his snip reversal! Pete soon recovered from the shock and managed to get a photo of James as the medical team worked on him.

I hadn't seen James's face when he was wheeled past me as his head was turned the other way. But I managed to reach out and touch his hand for a brief moment before he was hurried away. Then he was gone, the medical team taking him straight to the neonatal unit, a pumped-up Pete following on.

I was taken to the recovery room, but I was wired myself, and just kept jabbering on to some poor bloke who was supposed to be taking notes ... But I didn't want to be here, I wanted to be with my baby – I desperately wanted to see him. But of course I had to be kept under close observation, what with the anaesthetic and surgery. That meant going on an open ward – I couldn't go back to the peace and quiet of the private room I'd booked.

Anybody who's been on a maternity ward, but who for some reason couldn't have her baby with her, will know how I felt. I lay there behind the curtains, hearing all the excited chatter from the other new mums and the congratulations from their visitors. 'She's just had her first feed!' 'He looks just like his dad did when he was a baby!' And the click-whirr of digital cameras going all the time, recording those first precious hours. I just hope they took better pictures than Pete did ...

By late afternoon I was determined to see my baby, come what may. Much to the nurses' surprise, I could get up – all those years doing aerobics had obviously paid off and I was pretty fit. I got into a wheelchair and was taken down to the neonatal unit for my first proper sight of James.

So tiny. Just three pounds, lying there in a kind of open incubator. It was still hard to see his face, with the ventilator attached to his mouth and nose. He couldn't be moved, so all I could do was lean over him and gently stroke his hands. What I could see of him looked perfect.

When I could stop gazing at him, I turned my mind to practicalities and asked the nurse, 'When will he be having his op?'

'When he's stable,' she said, 'probably in a couple of days.'

I couldn't stay with James long – I had to go back to the ward – but before I could drag myself away from him, a kind nurse gave me a digital photo she'd taken of him. It gave me something to cling to during that long night.

*

It was two days later that he was prepared for the trip to Great Ormond Street, the only hospital capable of such complex surgery on a tiny baby.

Getting him ready was a major operation in itself. It took about an hour and a half to transfer him to the ambulance, with all the wires and tubes attached to him. Pete and I hovered about, trying not to get in the way. The past two days had been a whirl of emotions for us – we hadn't known if our baby would be born alive. We were ecstatic when he was, but racked with anxiety about the ordeal ahead of him.

Before James left UCLH, another kind nurse took some Polaroids of him: James with his dad, James with his mum, James with both his mum and dad. ('Mum' ... I was still trying to take in the fact that I really was a mother!) Again, there was that unspoken thought that these pictures might be the final mementos of our son – you might think this sounds melodramatic, but we all knew that James faced a life-threatening procedure.

And in the midst of all this, I had a reminder of the power of the gutter press. Even here, in the case of a desperately sick baby and his distraught parents.

I realized that some of the Polaroids had gone astray among all the hubbub. The only people who could have taken them were two girls visiting another mum and baby – they were the only visitors at the time, and I'd seen them looking at me, whispering and nudging each other.

They must have pinched them. Why would they do that? Only to sell them.

I was so angry – I wouldn't rest. Pete and I persuaded the mum to give us her friends' phone number. We just wanted to give them a chance to return the photos. We left a message saying that if the pictures had accidentally fallen into a handbag, we quite understood, but would they please return them as they were the only pictures we had of our baby son. This wasn't strictly true – we did have a few others – but we wanted to pull at their heartstrings. How could they resist that? But they did.

Right. I insisted on phoning the police and reporting the theft. I got a crime reference number, and armed with this I phoned round the usual rags, telling them that if they were offered pictures of my baby, they were stolen property and they'd be arrested.

All the papers said they hadn't been offered anything, but then one magazine admitted they had been offered exclusive pictures of 'that Lynne Slater's baby all wired up to machines'. I told the police, who asked the magazine to pretend to buy them in order to entrap the girls. But no deal. The magazine said it would frighten off other – what would you call them? Contributors? So those two toerags got away with it.

Meanwhile, James had gone to Great Ormond Street, followed by Pete. I was by myself, a new mother without her baby, and my precious photos had been stolen. That's it! I'd had enough. By the time Pete got back, I was dressed, packed and ready to leave – to everyone's surprise. I just couldn't see the point of staying there if James was somewhere else.

Pete was full of the joys of Great Ormond Street – 'James has a massive room all to himself,' he said. I imagined one small cot in the middle of it. Anyway, size isn't everything, as we all know. The staff at UCLH's neonatal unit do a brilliant job even in cramped conditions – the rooms, in the basement, are tiny, with low ceilings, and what's more it's always boiling hot down there. A lot of the other hospital departments have moved to the spanking new state-of-the-art building in Euston Road. While the neonatal unit is waiting for its turn to move, every day the staff save the lives of babies sent there from all over the country.

Over the next six months, I got to know the unit and its dedicated staff very well. Then one day, I was watching *GMTV* when some women came on, complaining that the hospital's nurses were dirty and had given their babies MRSA. What? I was gobsmacked. True, it's an old hospital, and there are always germs about, but when I think how hard the nurses in the unit worked – helping babies that other hospitals couldn't even begin to treat – it made my blood boil. The nurses I saw were always washing their hands and it didn't seem right to point the finger. Those complaining women really pissed me off with their ingratitude. I looked at one of them with her inch-thick make-up and thought, 'I wouldn't be surprised if you'd infected your baby from your make-up bag!' Any criticism of those nurses gets short shrift from me.

Back to December and James's op. Of course that's the moment when you think you might lose them – so tiny, and the added danger of the anaesthetic. But it was a success, thank God, despite the hernia being very serious. The bowel – a very large organ – had grown right through into the chest cavity, severely restricting his left lung and displacing his heart. What's more, his stomach had been pushed the wrong way round, along with his appendix. I remember one of the surgeons, a lovely guy, saying to us after it was all over, 'We whipped out his appendix at the same time.' And why?

'It wouldn't do for him to be eighteen and on holiday in Paris with his friends – he gets a belly ache and nobody realizes it's his appendix because it's on the wrong side!' That's forward thinking for you.

James stayed in Great Ormond Street intensive care for over a week. Although the surgery had sorted out his abdominal organs, the damaged lung still needed a lot of help. Pete and I got into the routine of staying most of the day and then going home in the evening. On Christmas Eve, we went there with my great friend Tonny, who I'd known since those first *EastEnders* auditions. I'd asked her to be one of James's godmothers, along with Julie. The godfather was my cousin Kevin, my dad's nephew. He's more like a brother to me and Sophie, and we love him to bits. He's very camp, quite a drama queen, which helps a lot with the drag act he does in pubs and clubs. Some of Mum's old party dresses look really good on him! He never would have been the most conventional of godfathers … but he has a heart of gold, and like all our friends was devoted to James. I don't know what we would have done without such selfless support.

Back to Christmas Eve. One of the staff saw us hovering over the cot, and said, 'Haven't you held him yet?' When we said no, we'd just been holding his hands, giving him little kisses and changing his nappy, he said, 'Right, we'll have to sort that out.' Before long there were some complicated manoeuvres with equipment, and Pete and I were able to hold our son in our arms for the first time. We were euphoric, taking in every detail.

We wanted to know what colour his eyes were, but the lighting in the room was so dim that we couldn't be sure. 'They're blue.' 'No – definitely brown.' It seemed to take us for ever, but we finally agreed that they were blue. His eyelashes were extraordinarily long – you could have put curlers in them, just like my mum's. James definitely had a look of my dad about the face, too, with the same shape eyes and mouth.

Tonny had brought her camera, and took photos of us all. She said, 'Seeing James in your arms is the best Christmas present I could have had.' And that evening, the doctors felt he was well enough to transfer back to UCLH. Fantastic, we thought, real progress. Had we turned a corner?

After that joyful moment, though, there was another upset – the very next day, Christmas Day.

It started well. When we arrived that morning, it was to see him dressed for the first time. The staff had put him in a tiny babygro – until then, he hadn't worn anything but a nappy. And he was wearing a tiny Christmassy hat – he looked adorable! I couldn't wait to go straight out and buy up all the gorgeous little clothes I could lay my hands on.

But while we were there he had a funny turn – I didn't understand exactly what it was, but his breathing was difficult and he gave us all a scare. In a moment, doctors and nurses were around his cot, working on him.

Not that we knew it then, but this was setting the pattern for what was to come. James would make progress, then something would go wrong, then he'd rally, then he'd fall back again, then he'd have yet another delicate operation ... And all the time he battled to survive. We called him 'Our little fighter' (and, when he eventually began to put on weight, 'Our fatty chapatti'!).

James would be taken to Great Ormond Street for the ops, and then back to UCLH for aftercare. It became a way of life for Pete and me. I'd spend most of the day with James, at whichever hospital he was in, and Pete would join us after work. Then we'd go home – as we lived so close to both hospitals, it didn't seem fair to take up one of the parents' rooms, unless James's condition seemed particularly worrying. Sometimes Pete worked flexible hours and could spell me for an afternoon. I'd usually go round my sister's and promptly fall asleep. But Pete and I would always phone the ward every night before we went to bed.

After a while James was taken off the ventilator and helped to breathe by means of a c-pap – this stands for 'continuous positive airway pressure' (we were rapidly learning all the jargon). With this, he had tubes in his nose that delivered oxygen from a ventilator, but the crucial difference is this: the c-pap was helping him to breathe, but not breathing for him.

This meant James could be more mobile and have what's called 'kangaroo care' – I held him close to my chest, skin to skin, for as long as possible. This has all sorts of benefits. It's comforting for both mum and baby, and strengthens the bond between them. I loved the closeness, the intimacy.

Apart from the usual round of baby care, I also had to

learn how to give him his medications, and how to manage all his tubes and lines and feeding procedures (he was being fed through his nose at this point). The nurses showed me how to do it, then supervised me until I was confident enough to do it by myself. I'd never imagined doing these kinds of meticulous medical tasks, but it's amazing what you can do when you have to. In any case, naturally I wanted to do it. I wanted to do my best for James, and after all I'd be on my own at home – when he eventually got there.

Pete was learning all the routines too, of course. Pity there was one thing he couldn't help with, though – breast-feeding.

Not that James could have fed normally while he was on the ventilator. I had to express my milk, and what a job that was! I had a breast pump. I had one at home as well – and I hated it. It was bloody hard work, and the noise of the machine drove me mad – 'Pschee-oot, pschee-oot, pschee-oot …' What made it worse was that I didn't even have a lot to show for the effort. Pete once congratulated me extravagantly on producing 2ml. I must say I did find it all very stressing, though of course, as we all know, breast is best, so I had to persevere.

But I was upset early one morning when Pete took a phone call from someone at the hospital.

'They want to know whether you'd agree to James having donor milk,' he told me.

What? My immediate thought was, that's disgusting. The very idea of somebody else's milk in my baby! But then, as

Pete pointed out, it's no different from accepting donated blood, so in the end we agreed.

Meanwhile, James was having real problems with reflux, bringing up acid and the contents of his stomach. Babies with his condition often get reflux and it can be serious. Apart from being very upsetting in itself, there's a risk of aspiration, when fluid gets on to the lungs, which is extremely dangerous. It also means that all the feed isn't being properly digested so the baby doesn't gain weight. In the end James had to be switched from donated breast milk to a special high-nutrition formula.

As if poor James didn't have enough to cope with – it just didn't seem fair. By now, he'd had another hernia, in his stomach this time, and fortunately a small one. It was what's called an incisional hernia, caused during one of his surgical procedures. This was no reflection on the surgery, I hasten to add, it's a common hazard for small babies. Another operation fixed it, but it didn't help the reflux problem.

The doctors tried the simplest treatment first, slowing down his rate of feeding and hoping that his stomach would gradually adapt and cope with it. James didn't respond to this, though antacid medicine helped a little, for a while. He still wasn't gaining weight, though, and he really needed another operation, quite a major one, called the Nissen fundoplication. As the doctor explained, it involved attaching part of the stomach round the windpipe, to create a valve, which tightens everything up and stops the liquid rising.

Yet another operation. How much surgery can one tiny body take? But take it James did, and for a couple of weeks his condition improved and he was back in UCLH. Only for something else to go wrong, taking him back to Great Ormond Street again.

And we adapted, Pete and I, as you have to. After some months, we felt quite like old hands. In fact Professor Rodeck asked us if we would talk to couples whose unborn babies had been diagnosed with a diaphragmatic hernia, to give them an idea of what to expect. Of course we said yes – we were only too happy to pass on what we'd learned. We used to tell them that one of the most important pieces of advice we'd been given was to go and look round the neonatal unit before the baby's birth. As Pete and I had found, it's nerve-racking enough to see it with other people's babies. If you saw it for the first time when your own baby was there, it could freak you out entirely. Going there beforehand would at least get some of the unknown quantity out of the way.

Pete and I felt so much for these parents. We knew what they would be facing.

Not that it was all doom and gloom in intensive care. Everybody was in the same boat – babies and parents – and we gave each other a lot of support. We met some lovely people. It was like a little nursery. Sometimes a baby would come in just for a night or two – we called them 'short-termers' – we were the lifers! Well, it felt like it anyway. Those of us who were together for weeks or months at a time built up a camaraderie. We used to chat, holding our babies, swap stories, help each when we could. One day a mum would be crying, and someone would comfort her, then the next day she'd be up and comfort someone else. We all needed support, locked into what seemed an endless, relentless round. But we even found things to laugh at.

There was one time when a baby was brought in, and he seemed huge – *huge*! What's he doing here? the rest of us wondered. Is it because he's too large? Poor boy. He turned out to be the normal size for a newborn. Us mums had got used to our tiny babies, mostly premature, and this new baby seemed practically old enough for school!

One thing that struck Pete and me at the time was that, despite all the desperately ill babies, it was rare for one of them not to make it. I remember one lovely couple whose baby was in the cot next to James. She was getting worse and worse, and eventually she had to be taken off the ventilator. The atmosphere changed instantly. It brought it home to all of us why we were there – death happens. Everybody cried. Everybody felt it. Of course, it could have been any of us ... The mum asked the nurse to tell us – she couldn't face doing it herself.

So we appreciated the good times all the more. We loved giving James his bath every day, and he loved it too – a real water baby. It was great when my mum and dad visited. Mum was still living in Matthews Court, just a short tube ride away. Dad was still living in Stevenage. His condition was gradually worsening, but like his grandson, Dad's a fighter. He was still mobile, and his devoted partner Eileen drove him down. By this stage, Dad's condition was making him shake, like Parkinson's, and when he held his grandson, James seemed to like the vibration! We later got him his own little massage chair.

It was lovely to see my mum and dad with their first grandchild. They doted on him, of course, but I could see my mum especially was getting upset. I thought this was natural, worrying about him, and worrying about me worrying about him! Mothers always worry …

Another great time was when Pete's children visited. They adored their little brother, and happily helped to give him a bath. Pete's elder daughter, then aged eleven, was a real little mother hen, and quickly learned to help with James's feeding and medication. Pete's son, with two sisters, was only too happy to have a brother at last.

As the months passed, I almost forgot any other life I may have had before. I got to know all the medical staff, even the security guards, who used to wave me through without signing me in, as I was such a familiar face, turning up every day. There were moments of sheer happiness, when James kicked, gurgled and smiled like any other baby, and days of sheer anxiety as yet another operation became necessary.

One momentous evening, we phoned the ward as usual before going to bed, and the doctor said, 'Ah, I was just about to phone you …' What followed started to feel like a nightmare. This doctor started rambling on – 'He had fluid on the lung, which we've had to aspirate, but unfortunately the procedure didn't work and we had to try ...' He went into further details, ' ... and then the baby pulled out the tube ...' I was hopping up and down while he burbled on ... 'And then we had to try blah blah ...' till I finally screamed, 'IS HE ALIVE?'

A shocked silence, then a quiet, 'Yes, but we suggest you come in.'

Right, we were off – on one of the worst journeys we ever had. Not because there was a tangle of traffic like there was during the day. Quite the opposite. It was around midnight, and the roads were eerily quiet. There was little to distract us from the fear and dread in our hearts. By the time we arrived at UCLH we were sweating. We dashed into intensive care, to see Jane – Dr Hawdon – the head of the neonatal unit, bent over James's cot, squeezing an air bag – in, out ... in, out ...

When she heard us come in, she glanced over her shoulder and flashed us a quick smile. I hoped to God it was a reassuring smile.

A short while later, when Pete and I were in a fit state to take anything in, she explained that she'd been called in after all attempts to insert an air line had failed. She'd managed to insert the tiniest, thinnest line into him, to keep his airways open – a tribute, we knew, to her vast experience. Thankfully, James had lost no oxygen, and he was transferred yet again to Great Ormond Street, where a proper-sized tube could be inserted while he was anaesthetized. One more life-saving operation.

*

So that's the kind of rollercoaster we got used to. We didn't miss a day with James – until something happened that took us away from him for a while. Something that was so huge, so terrible – I hadn't seen it coming. Focused as I was on the life of my son, desperately hoping that he might live, dreading every day that he might die, I hadn't seen death coming from another direction – towards the first love of my life. My mum.

CHAPTER EIGHT

Love and Loss

The questions never end. Why did it happen? How did it happen? Could it have been prevented? What else could those who loved her have done? Did we not do enough? What's the truth? Will we ever know?

My sister and I have gone over and over Mum's life. We have our own memories, of course, and she and Dad talked a lot about their early years together. We thought that perhaps if we kept going over Mum's life, we might find some answers.

*

It seems right that someone with so much heart should have been born on St Valentine's Day, the 14th of February. It was in 1943, and Bernie was the youngest of seven children born to Julia and William O'Regan. She grew up in Enniskeane in Cork, which Sophie and I would later get to know when we went on holiday there. By the time she was born, her future husband was already seven years and one week old. Garrett was born on the 7th of February 1936, and was also one of seven children, born to Julia and Charlie

Lordan. He grew up in the town of Clonakilty, which Sophie and I would also get to know.

Bernie and Garrett met when she was one week away from her sixteenth birthday. (I'm calling them Bernie and Garrett now, as they're not my mum and dad yet). They met in O'Donovan's Hotel in Clonakilty, at one of the regular dances held there. Bernie was a gorgeous-looking girl, with long dark hair and soulful brown eyes. She was always beautifully dressed, and that evening she'd borrowed a frock from her sister Kathleen, who had a good job working for a doctor and could afford nice things. 'It was love at first sight for me,' Garrett would always say. Their first dance was to 'When It's Springtime in the Rockies' by American country singer Slim Whitman – one of their special songs for ever after.

They met again at the next dance, in March, by which time Bernie was sweet sixteen. Garrett had a motorbike, which he was very proud of, and offered to give her a lift home. Bernie had to ask her brothers, who were also at the dance – this was the 1950s, remember – and they spoke to Garrett before agreeing. They were very protective of their little sister.

It was the first time Bernie had been on a motorbike, and she loved the wind in her hair and on her face. She wasn't so keen on the noise the bike made, though – it was deafening. Her brothers followed by car, her brother DP (Dennis Patrick) driving. When they all arrived at the O'Regan home, the brothers agreed that Garrett was a careful driver, so he had their seal of approval. Bernie and Garrett started going out together regularly. I remember Nanny O'Regan talking about the time when they were courting – 'We could hear the motorbike comin' from miles away!'

By the time they'd been going out for about a year, it was obvious they were made for each other, very much in love. But Bernie was barely seventeen and had never been out of Ireland. She had an adventurous spirit and wanted to see something of the world before settling down, so when her married sister Mary, who was living in Bexhill-on-Sea, invited her over to stay, Bernie jumped at the chance (well, Bexhill is part of the world). She sailed over, settled in, and got herself a job in a local Woolworth's.

And where Bernie went, Garrett followed. To London, at least. He'd already worked in London, as a bricklayer, and this time he took a room in Kilburn, that great magnet for Irish immigrants, and got another job in the building trade. He wanted to get married as soon as possible, so he got an evening job, too, in a bar. Working hard all week, he got a bit lonely, but he made up for it at weekends when he went to Bexhill to see Bernie. They'd walk along the beach by the pavilion like all the other young lovers, and plan their wedding day.

Near the time, Bernie left Bexhill to live with Garrett in Kilburn, working in another shop – I don't think the folks back home were aware that they were living in sin. Though they were saving as much money as possible, they did treat themselves to a night out once a week at the Galtymore Irish

Dance Hall in Kilburn High Road – they both loved dancing.

Their wedding day finally arrived, Saturday the 28th of April 1962. Bernie was nineteen. She looked stunning in her white dress, showing off her tiny waist and shapely legs. Garrett was handsome in his best suit. After the ceremony, in a church beautifully decorated with flowers, the newly-weds and all their guests went to the reception in the Connaught Rooms, a pub in Kilburn. 'She shall have a really special day,' Garrett had declared, 'no expense spared.' So they had a lavish wedding feast and a good time was had by all.

Then Bernie and Garrett started married life.

*

That's the bare bones of my parents' love story. I used to love hearing it, how my mum and dad got together before they were my mum and dad. I'd look at the old photos, at their wedding album, and imagine their life together. Then I'd hear the rest of it – how Bernie quickly became pregnant and they were both over the moon. Bernie worked till she was seven and a half months pregnant. Garrett wasn't keen on her working, but Bernie knew they would need all the money they could get. Sophie was born on the 14th of June 1963, and all three of them lived in the rented room in Kilburn. It was quite hard for Bernie, with a baby at twenty and no family nearby, but she was always a grafter and made the best of it. And because she was warm-hearted and generous, she soon made friends.

Then they heard of a bigger bedsit off the Holloway Road. When they viewed it, they took it straight away. There was another room vacant, and Bernie's brother DP, who'd also come over to work, took it. It was about this time that he started showing symptoms of the arthritis that would cripple him.

One day there was a drama – Sophie stopped breathing. Bernie grabbed her from her cot and ran, clutching her to her chest, past the Archway and up Highgate Hill, all the way to the Whittington Hospital, where mercifully the doctors were able to save Sophie. I'd listen to this story with tears in my eyes, knowing my mum was a heroine.

Bernie fell pregnant again, this time with me, and there was the nail-biting process of getting the flat in Highbury Hill – it wasn't until the day Mum came out of hospital with me that it was confirmed they'd got it. So now I was born, and Bernie and Garrett were Mum and Dad. A very satisfying story, I always thought, ending with my arrival.

There was something missing in this story, though, and I didn't learn about it until I was about eleven years old. What I was told turned my world upside down. Later on, when I grew up, I wondered if it had had the same effect on Mum.

*

It was a Sunday lunchtime. Mum and Dad had had one of their rows and the atmosphere was heavy. Dad went off to the pub, and when he got back he wasn't drunk – he rarely was – but he wanted to get a dig in at Mum.

Dad called me into the kitchen, where Mum was cooking, and said to me, 'If there was a family secret and everybody knew it except you, would you want to know?'

What? What brought this on? What's he talking about? Then it suddenly hit me, Oh my God, I'm adopted! I promptly ran off to the front room and burst into tears. Now this was really bizarre – I'd no reason at all to think I was adopted. Perhaps it was just the worst thing my young self could imagine, not really being the daughter of Mum and Dad.

Then I pulled myself together. Well, I thought, if I am adopted, I need to know. So I braced myself and walked back into the kitchen.

'Yeah, I do wanna know,' I told him. 'What is it, this secret?'

Mum was leaning against the sink, her hand on her head, with a look that said, oh no, here it comes.

Dad turned to me. 'You have a brother,' he announced.

What? Another puzzle. How could I have a brother? Did Dad mean Mum had had a baby and I hadn't noticed?

He elaborated. 'Your mother had a baby boy years ago. I wanted to keep him but your mother didn't. She gave him away. But he's your brother.'

This was too incredible to take in. I looked wildly from one to the other, and to Sophie, who was sitting at the table. 'Did you know about this?' I demanded. Sophie nodded. 'Yeah.'

This was even worse. Everybody knew but me. On top of the shock was the fact that I'd been left out. I don't know what hurt more. I remember yelling at my mum, 'You bitch!' God help me, that was awful, me saying that to my mother. Then I ran out of the kitchen and upstairs to my room, where I fell on the bed and cried buckets.

A short while later, Mum came up. She sat on the bed, held my hand and said, 'It wasn't the way yer dad said it was. It was different. There was a baby and he did go away, but it wasn't like yer dad said.'

My mind was in turmoil. I loved my mum so much – to think she hadn't shared such a big thing with me was so hurtful! Then a twitch of jealousy that Sophie should know before me ...

What I couldn't understand at the time was how my mum, the most loving mum in the world, could give up a baby. How could she do such a thing? Didn't she love the baby? Of course I was thinking like the young child I was. Black and white. Later, I'd cringe as I remembered how I used to climb into bed with her on Saturday mornings for a cuddle. I'd say to her, 'Why don't you have another baby, Mum? Oh, go on. I'd love a little brother – have another baby, go on.' I can't imagine what that would have been like for her. She must have been really hurt, even though I spoke in all innocence.

For me, the shock waves from this thunderbolt took some time to die down. Eventually I pieced the picture together.

Bernie found out she was pregnant while she was still living with her sister Mary in Bexhill. She couldn't believe it when the doctor told her. She wasn't even sure that she'd actually done the dirty deed, which says a lot about sex education in Ireland in the Fifties. Mum was very innocent, and she was in shock. Being Catholic, there was no question of an abortion – and in those days they weren't easy to get anyway. And there was the shame – she couldn't bring shame on her family. There was no question of marriage yet, as they had nothing to live on. So secrecy was the order of the day. Apparently her sister Mary noticed a difference in Bernie – 'Are you not puttin' on a bit o' weight?' she asked. But in her first pregnancy Bernie didn't show much, and she kept on working in Woolworth's. If Mary had her suspicions, she kept quiet. Certainly not a whisper would get back to the family in Cork.

It was when the baby's birth drew near that Bernie joined Garrett in Kilburn and made the arrangements. She would have the baby in a London hospital, and then take him or her over to Dublin, to a Catholic unmarried mothers' home, to stay there for a few weeks while she recovered and decided, along with Garrett, what to do for the future.

She had the baby, a boy – 'the most beautiful baby I've ever seen,' she said – and took him, alone, over to Ireland on the boat. The nuns took the baby and gave Bernie papers to sign, which she duly did. She then said to them, 'Right, I'll be back in six weeks when I've sorted myself out.'

'Oh no you won't,' they said. 'You've signed the papers giving him up for good. You've no rights over him any more.'

This was a hammer blow for Bernie. She tried to protest,

but the home was adamant, and the circumstances difficult. As she told me, she felt she'd been cruelly misled somewhere along the line. Later, I did wonder if she hadn't fully understood the implications of what she was signing. After all, she was young, naïve – and alone. What is certain is that Bernie would never knowingly have given up her baby. She just wanted time to rest and sort things out.

She never had a hope of contesting the decision. She had no money for a lawyer, and anyway, going to the law wasn't for the likes of her. That was for the rich, the educated.

Bernie dragged herself back to London and told Garrett what had happened. He went berserk, blaming her. It must have been devastating for both of them, and a secret that could never go beyond our immediate family. Years later, I was to go to the funeral of one of Mum's sisters, who died a year or so after Mum. It was then that I told her surviving brothers, and nobody had heard a word about it before. It's sad that Mum felt she couldn't tell her wider family, even after times had moved on in Ireland.

When Mum's story sunk in, I used to question her all the time: 'Didn't you go and look for him?'

She would say that basically, she had to accept the fact that he wasn't hers any more. She'd have to trust the nuns to place him in a good home, where his new parents would love him as much as she would have. I think in her mind she worked up a bit of a fantasy, that he'd gone to a rich family and was now a doctor or something equally prestigious. She used to say that she'd have loved to see him, but from a distance, as a family friend, say. She would never have dreamed of intruding on his life and announcing herself as his birth mother: 'That just wouldn't be fair, now.'

But it didn't stop her thinking about him every day of her life.

*

Was it this loss, this loss of her first child, that ate into Mum all those years? With guilt adding to the anguish? When Sophie and I were kids, there was never any sign of an underlying sadness, an inexplicable melancholy – though perhaps we would have been too young to pick up on subtleties. Then again, when we grew up she seemed to be the same strong, grounded, warm-hearted woman. Positive and encouraging – and so good-humoured. She didn't mope in corners, she was the life and soul of any party, such a laugh, Aunty Mary used to say she could have been a comedian.

Talking of which, Mum had brilliant comic timing – she'd crease us up with funny stories, real stories, that happened at work. There was one time I remember, she was working part-time in King's Bakeries in Highbury Barn, preparing rolls and sandwiches and selling them in the shop. By now Islington was going a bit upmarket, more money was coming in and the middle classes were making their presence felt. One day, Mum was serving a posh bloke his wholemeal loaf when Vera the cleaner wandered by. Now Vera was one of the old school, a traditional cockney whose family had lived in the area for ever. She always called a spade a spade –

a fuckin' shovel, in fact – and always said the first thing that came into her head. This time, as Mum was serving the customer, Vera lifted up her broom and showed Mum how threadbare it was. ''Ere, Bern,' said Vera, 'look at this bleedin' broom. I got more 'airs on me prat.'

And Mum would enact perfectly her own embarrassment, Vera's complete obliviousness, and the posh customer's recoil of disgust. We could practically see it all!

Mum obviously took such pleasure in life, so when she said she thought of the baby every day, it might have been with a kind of detached fondness, not a grief that tore at her. Then again, being the unselfish person she was, Mum could simply have been hiding what she felt, not wanting to worry anyone.

It wasn't until she took the overdose in 1999 that we suspected anything was wrong. She did have another attempt, three years later, which frightened the life out of everybody, but again, thank God, it seemed half-hearted, as if she was going through the motions rather than really intending to go through with it. She told Sophie and me that she'd taken a load of pills and we took her to the doctor. He didn't think she needed to go to hospital. Looking back, I don't know why we didn't insist she had specialized help, though after Sophie's experience in the mental hospital, Mum wouldn't have been keen to go.

Mum had been very supportive to Sophie when she had depression years before. She was more patient than me. 'If Sophie had a broken leg, now,' she'd say, 'anybody would help her across the road and think nothing of it. But something wrong with the mind – that's just an embarrassment. People can't see it, often don't believe it. They're livin' in the dark ages!' That's true enough. But as I've said before, I can't pretend to have a great understanding of depression. My old friend Anna Scher would say, about her own breakdown, that it's all so mysterious – where does depression come from? Why do some suffer and not others? Chemical imbalance, genetics? I don't know. All I've learned is that the suffering is very real.

*

Could it have been her relationship with Dad that tipped Mum over? Talk about tempestuous … Long years of suspicion and jealousy on Dad's part could have worn her down. If you'd seen them when they were fighting, hammer and tongs, you'd have thought they hated each other. And perhaps at that moment they did. But at heart they were both hot-blooded and passionately in love, I see that now.

I've said before that Dad was very jealous where Mum was concerned. She was so beautiful, men always clustered around her, and she did delight in flirting. That's as far as it went, I'm sure of that, but it was like a red rag to a bull for my dad. He was on a hair trigger – anything could set him off.

There was one time that reverberated around the family for weeks. Mum and Dad had gone out for the evening, while Maureen next door babysat me and Sophie. Debbie must have been with us too. In the taxi home – they could afford such luxuries by now – Dad thought he could see the driver ogling Mum in the rear-view mirror. It must be said that Mum was wearing a miniskirt, fashionable at the time. Now this skirt was nothing like the pelmets girls wear these days – it was not much above the knee, worn with very smart boots. Mum was always classy.

Dad got it into his head that the cabbie was leching after his wife, and addressed him in typical Dad style. 'You take yer feckin' eyes off my wife now! I've seen yer, starin' at her legs!'

When the cabbie said he wasn't, Dad erupted. 'How dare you feckin' stare at my wife's legs, you feckin' pervert – pull over an' I'll teach you some manners.'

Mum tried to keep the peace, but in vain. A very acrimonious journey ended outside our door with Dad paying the driver and telling him to piss off – which he did, sharpish.

Mum remonstrated with Dad, and that's when an almighty row started. It culminated in such a scene in the kitchen ... Mum had bought a beautiful Welsh dresser, and on the shelves she'd displayed some lovely blue and white plates that her sister Mary had given her. Well, Dad was in such a rage that he wrenched the dresser bodily to the floor, smashing all the plates. Chaos. At least the violence was confined to the dresser. Like most men of his background, Dad did hit out at Mum when things got out of hand – when he lost his rag and lashed out in temper. He wasn't like it all the time, of course. When he was in a good humour there wasn't a kinder, more tender-hearted man. But the violence was part of the culture back then. You'd often hear ructions coming from the other flats in the house, too – angry words, screams, the sound of objects being thrown against doors.

Sometimes Dad's reactions were so over the top he seemed unbalanced, working himself into a right lather about Mum's goings-on, real or imaginary. One time it even involved the police. It's a long story, but it says a lot about my mum and dad's relationship when things went off the rails.

One night, Mum and her mate Maureen were working late in the pub – there was a special function. I don't know whether it'd been sprung on them, or whether Mum had forgotten to tell Dad (he was at home looking after me and Sophie). Maureen drove them both home, and went indoors. Mum tried to do the same, but found the door locked. She rang the bell, but Dad wouldn't answer. She rang and rang, but no result. So she sat on the garden wall, wondering what to do.

Eventually she decided to climb in through the big front window – something me and Sophie would do for a laugh. You had to climb on to a ledge from the front steps, and balance on the windowsill while you opened the window. Now Mum was no good at climbing, and was frightened of falling – perhaps it was a memory of breaking her arm in Spain when she fell off the fence (or rather when Dad pushed her over it). Dad must have been listening out for her, though, because as soon as she managed to perch on the windowsill, he ran into the front room and locked the window before she could open it.

Mum knocked on the window, but Dad just laughed – 'So yer've been out workin' till this time! Yer must think I'm a fool – yer not comin' in here! That'll teach ya, yer tart – yer takin' the fuckin' piss!'

Mum pleaded with him, but he wouldn't let her in. He was really working himself into a ferocious temper. He just kept laughing and then pulled the curtains across.

So now Mum was stuck. She managed to lower herself onto the ledge and sit on it, but she didn't dare jump off. It wasn't a long drop to the ground, but she was too scared to move. If it was me, I'd have kicked the glass in, but Mum could never be violent. She sat there for an hour or so, until a couple of people walked by. She called to them – but quietly, so she wouldn't disturb the neighbours. 'Excuse me, could you help me, please?'

The couple came over – they were American, very nice. Mum explained what had happened, and they were shocked. She asked them to keep ringing the bell, and the man obliged. Dad eventually opened the door, and the American woman said, 'We're sorry to wake you, but your wife is on the window ledge and the window is locked. Could you open it, please, and let her in?'

Dad stepped out, looked at Mum and said, 'I've never seen that woman before in my life. I've no idea who she is and I most certainly will not let her into my house.'

Turning to the American couple, he said, 'Don't ring my bell again,' and shut the door.

Mum was saying, 'Garrett, Garrett, stop this, see reason …' but Dad ignored her.

The couple were even more shocked. The man said to Mum, 'Are you sure you live here, ma'am?'

'Yes, of course I do,' said Mum. 'That man is my husband and right now he's a ravin' lunatic. What am I goin' to do?'

This poor couple – suddenly presented with such madness! The man suggested that Mum climbed off the ledge and down the steps – he helped her do it. Now what?

'Shall we call the police?' asked the woman. No, said Mum, she'd try the bell again.

'Shall we wait?' the Americans asked.

'No, thank you,' said Mum. 'I'll be all right now.'

They looked a bit doubtful, but moved away. Mum rang and rang the bell, but got no reply, so eventually she made a decision. She walked to the phone box on the corner and rang the police.

Before long two officers, a man and a woman, arrived. Mum explained the situation, and this time the policeman rang the bell … for a long time. Dad finally opened the door.

'What's going on here?' asked the policeman. 'You've locked your wife out and won't let her back in. What do you think you're doing?'

'Me?' said Dad, all injured innocence. 'I've been sleepin', that's what I've been doin'. That one' – jerking his head at

Mum – 'she's always out late drinkin'. Forgot yer keys again, did ya?'

Mum was livid, on top of being tired out.

'Garrett!' she said. 'You're a lunatic. I'll not talk to you any more.' She walked in through the door and the police followed. They chose to believe Dad's version of events and told Mum off for wasting everybody's time. Mum wasn't having any of that.

After Dad had stomped off upstairs to bed, Mum said to the policemen, 'You just wait here and I'll prove how mad he is. I'll open and close the front door and he'll think you've gone.'

When she'd done this, the police hid behind the front room door. Dad ran down the stairs in his underpants and walked into the room, laughing maniacally. 'That'll teach ya!' he jeered. 'Did ya enjoy yer time on the ledge, then?'

The police showed themselves. 'What did you mean by that?' they asked.

Dad was speechless. Mum said, 'I told you, he's a madman. I've been workin' all day, until late at night, and I'm tired. Then he has to do this jealous rage stuff – all because he doesn't want me workin' and earnin' me own money. You're crazy, Garrett.'

The police asked Dad what he had to say for himself.

'She's makin' it all up,' he said. 'She's been out drinkin' all night.'

Now the police came down on Mum's side. 'Why don't you leave your wife alone and go to bed? Then we'll be able to leave as well.'

Dad stomped back up the stairs, and the police stayed until Mum was sure Dad was asleep. Only then could she relax and sleep herself. Next morning – well, talk about hammer and tongs. Dad started, telling Mum he'd come to the conclusion that she was seeing another man.

'Oh, Garrett, don't be ridiculous. I don't give a damn about your bloody conclusion – I've reached me own, and it's that yer stark ravin' mad. Just cos yer don't want me to have some independence, to have a life outside the home.'

'What? Don't I give you enough money, is that it?'

'No, yer not listenin'. I want me own money so I can have me own bit of independence. Look at last night, that was stupid. I know it was late, but it's all extra money – can yer not understand that? For Christ's sake, let's put it behind us.'

'No I can't, and I wasn't the stupid one last night. I was treatin' you the way you deserved.'

'Oh, don't talk such rubbish. Me and Maureen don't work late that often, but when we do, you always have to pick a fight—'

'Don't talk to me about Maureen – I've seen, I can tell, she's up to it as well, you're both up to it—'

'Oh, that's it! I've had enough of this, why don't you piss off to the pub and give us all some peace. You're upsettin' the girls, and over nothin' at all! I have seriously had enough, Garrett, so do me a favour and give me some space.'

*

It sounds like a madhouse, doesn't it? I suppose most families have their own version of these long-running arguments, when all kinds of stuff get raked up and nothing gets sorted. The thing is, as I've already said, when Dad's rage died down, there wasn't a kinder, more generous man in the world. He was so devoted to his family, so hardworking, such good fun. Despite the domestic violence – which we deplore these days and quite right too – Dad did have a heart of gold, his basic instincts were solid. Just one example, when I was a baby and wouldn't have known about it, but everyone told me later.

It was late, one dark night. Everything was quiet. Suddenly a woman's screams rang out – coming from Highbury Fields, just beyond our garden wall. Lights went on, people opened windows – and when my dad realized what was happening, he was off like a shot. Bounded down the stairs in his bare feet, rushed down the back garden, scrambled over the wall, and dropped down into the fields. He ran towards the sound of screaming, and found a woman on the ground with a man trying to rape her. Dad leaped on the man, hauled him off and hit him hard. The bastard ran off and Dad helped the woman up. He walked her round to our house, and got the police. Next day, the woman came round to thank him. He was a hero.

Aren't some people complicated? Or as Mum said of Dad, 'He's a mass of contradictions all right.'

Apart from his jealousy and his resentment about Mum earning her own money, I wonder if the loss of their first baby was also behind Dad's anger. Did he blame Mum for it entirely? Did he truly regret it? Or did he just use it as a weapon?

There's another thing as well. Perhaps it rankled with Dad that he hadn't had the education he deserved. Everyone always felt that he was very intelligent. It was Dad who spent hours playing Scrabble and such-like with me as a child – this is what developed my love of language and words. He shone at school, was always the first with his hand up. He read a lot, had a great interest in knowledge, and the teachers said he'd be a natural for grammar school. But that was out of the question. There was no money for the uniform, and in any case he had to leave school as soon as possible to start earning money. That was the usual fate in those days for boys and girls from working-class backgrounds, no matter how great their potential. So Dad went the way of many of his compatriots and became a bricklayer. He was a very good brickie, too, and was much in demand, but it must have been frustrating for him to know that he could have gone to university – he certainly had the intellect for it.

I do know that he was so proud when Sophie went to secondary school, Barnsbury School for Girls – there was no question of not affording the uniform! So Sophie was kitted out in the regulation green pleated skirt with a red sash, white shirt, green tie and blazer. And Dad bought her what he would have loved himself – a big, posh briefcase, an expensive one from John Lewis. But of course Sophie didn't want it – all the other girls had ordinary school bags, and she felt so embarrassed. Dad meant well, but it was his dream, not hers.

Whatever the root of Dad's temper, it wasn't as if Mum couldn't fight back, in her way. As well as a quick tongue, she was smart. If she wanted to, she could needle right back, as she told me.

One New Year's Eve, when I was away with friends and Sophie had left home to travel in the USA, Mum and Dad were alone in Matthews Court. There was a row – I don't know the precise cause – and they weren't talking. Then at half past eleven Dad announced he was going to the pub to see the new year in and so there.

Mum was left sitting on the sofa, thinking, you bastard. Then she had a mischievous thought. Sophie had bought her some sexy underwear for Christmas, and Mum took the bra and knickers out of the wrapper and ran them under the tap in the bathroom. She then arranged them on the clothes airer over the bath, and went back to the sofa.

Dad came back from the pub a bit worse for wear – it was New Year's Eve so he'd had more than a few – and went to the toilet, which was also in the bathroom. Before long, he burst out the door. 'What's this? You've feckin' well been out, haven't you! What? What? What?'

That got her a slap, but Mum didn't care. She'd got to him. She wouldn't, couldn't, hurt him physically, but she'd give him a metaphorical kick in the balls.

When there was a final parting of the ways, I think it was

Mum's initiative. Perhaps she wanted a quieter life – trade the passion and drama for tranquillity. She was always the peaceful one. She and Dad had been married for about twenty-five years, and perhaps that was enough for them, although they never actually got divorced. Dad moved out of the flat in Matthews Court and found a place of his own nearby. For a while, he couldn't accept the break, couldn't tear himself away.

I remember one time, I must have been about twenty-three and was still living in Matthews Court. I'd been out clubbing and got home around four in the morning. There was something, a shape, outside the main door to the flats. It looked like an extended sun lounger, with someone on it, covered by a quilt. I peered closely at the figure and lifted the quilt. It was my dad! Oh, this is ridiculous, I thought. I got my key out, opened the door and went upstairs. Mum was awake, so I said, 'Mum, he's out there.' And she said, 'I know.'

'Aren't you worried about him?' I asked. (I who had just blithely ignored him and gone up the stairs.)

'Don't you worry about him,' said Mum. 'It's just one of his demonstrations.' I loved the way she pronounced it – 'dee-mon-strations' – making Dad sound like a demon!

He was proving a point, but to no avail. Mum did wonder if she could ever take him back – at one time she thought she could, when they were friends again – but no. It was all too much. It was impossible for them to live together.

But she'd be the first to say the good times were the best. And he was a truly wonderful dad, and still is.

*

Do we make progress? Are we any nearer finding the root cause of whatever it was that affected Mum? Probably not.

Mum went on living in the flat, and Dad stayed in his new place for a while. He eventually found a new partner – they met in Clonakilty as it happened, when she was on holiday and Dad was visiting his family. The first I knew of it was when I went round to his flat after I'd had a row with my then boyfriend. Dad was always a good listener, always comforting. I was bending his ear in the living room when I caught a glimpse of something thrown over the back of a chair. It was a bra.

'Dad,' I said, 'what's that bra doing there? Either you've turned into a cross-dresser or there's a woman around.'

Just then, a woman came in from the bedroom, and that was my first sight of Eileen. They later moved to Stevenage where, towards the end of the 1990s, Dad was diagnosed with progressive supranuclear palsy, which has no cure. But he's outlived his prognosis. The doctors told us that most people don't last five years with the condition, and Dad's still battling after seven, with devoted care from Eileen. The shaking is bad now, and he has to be fed, but his brain remains lucid – he recognizes people and can still get words out, with an effort. You still get flashes of the old spirit. He never complains – he's showing a different kind of heroism now.

Thinking of Dad's spirit reminds me how much it matters to keep that zest for life, to be stimulated. One day Pete and I visited Mum's sister Kathleen, who was living in an old people's home. Kathleen and the other residents were just sitting there, in their high-backed chairs, their heads lolling, eyes blank, the telly blaring away in the background. Kathleen recognized us, after a fashion, but her personality hardly seemed to be there any longer. It was as if there was some kind of bad spell imprisoning all the old folk. Pete and I then got an idea into our heads – 'Go for it!' And we did our speciality dance act in front of them, ending in a spectacular back flip, with me flying over Pete's head and landing behind him. We took a bow in front of the audience and noticed that most people had lifted their heads and were smiling. One old bloke was even clapping – well, moving his trembling hands together.

Pete and I could have cried. The life force was still there – it just has to be kept going (with rather more help than our mad dance act, of course).

Meanwhile Mum was rebuilding her life in Matthews Court. She made the flat lovely, got herself a part-time job and seemed as happy as ever. Perhaps with my dad away she could relax more. She certainly had a busy social life, and was her usual helpful self to friends and neighbours. She took a special interest in the old bloke upstairs, Jack, who couldn't get out. She'd get his shopping – and she was still taking care of Uncle DP until he got so bad that he had to go into a nursing home. And she met a new man, the lovely Doug.

She and Dad remained friends, though, and he and Eileen would sometimes come to London, and Mum would put on a lovely spread for them.

Mum was always supportive of Sophie and me, in good times and bad. She helped Sophie through her depression, and when I joined *EastEnders* she was happy for me when things were going well and commiserated when they weren't. I have a very special memory of taking her to one of those TV awards ceremonies – where they give prizes to anything from sexiest newcomer to the knobbliest knees in a soap. Not my cup of tea, but Mum did love the glitz. She was beautifully dressed herself, and could hardly take her eyes off Joan Collins – 'Will you look at her now,' she breathed, 'such style, such glamour …' I'm so glad she enjoyed herself.

When I was pregnant, I took my eye off the ball where Mum was concerned. Along with Pete, I focused all my concerns and energy on the baby. And when James was born, there was the constant attention to his needs. I hope this doesn't sound like excuses. I'm afraid I left Mum to Sophie, who always looked out for her – as much as Mum would let her, at least.

We sometimes wonder whether it was my having James that affected Mum badly. Brought back memories of the baby she had to give up – a boy, of course. I can hardly bear to think that my baby could have triggered off her actions.

But now we get to the sequence of events that can be proved, substantiated.

James was only a month or so old when Mum started to behave … differently. As if she'd lost focus. She seemed to be getting a bit confused, forgetful. We can all sympathize with that. But something seemed to have gone out of Mum – her spark, her buoyant spirit.

Was this classic depression? She did go to the doctor, and was prescribed pills. I'm not sure what they were – probably anti-depressants. She complained of not being able to sleep, and started drinking heavily. Mum had never been a drinker. She enjoyed it, sure, but hardly ever overdid it. Now she was seriously attacking the vodka.

She was also restless, couldn't relax. Sophie was trying to look after her, but Mum resisted. By early March of the new year (we're now in 2005), the change in her was really marked. In a shockingly short time she'd gone from the woman we knew to almost – well, like a child. Somebody who would drift around, hardly able to do anything for herself. She would come round to our flat just as Pete and I were going to visit James, and – God forgive me – we'd lock her in. We just didn't think she'd be safe out on her own. She began to say, again and again, 'I've lost it, I've lost it.' Lost what, Mum? She meant her mind.

And where were the doctors meanwhile? Sophie had been to see the GP, to beg for something to be done for Mum. Change the medication, give her something to help her sleep – do something! I think he may have prescribed something, but if he did it didn't seem to help.

Then on the 17th of March, Mum took another overdose.

Again not enough to kill her, thank God, but surely nothing could be clearer as a cry for help? It was St Patrick's Day, a special day for the Irish – did she feel abandoned, isolated? Sophie was desperately trying to get the medical authorities to do something. On the 21st of March she managed to get Mum into the Drayton Park Women's Crisis Centre, just round the corner. This is a kind of clinic, a refuge for women with urgent mental health needs. God, it's a five-minute walk away, but I didn't go there. I was desperately worried about Mum, guilty that I was leaving everything to Sophie, but I was trying so hard to concentrate on James. And I had the horrible thought that if I visited the centre, I'd be spotted, and the tabloids would say something vile – EX-SOAP STAR'S MUM IN LOONY BIN. If Mum ever got wind of something like that, it'd hardly help her recovery. So I left the flat only to go to see James. I so regret it now.

Thursday the 24th of March. The usual routine. Pete went to work, and I went to see James. I spent the day with him, doing the usual things, seeing to his feeds, bathing him and so on, and waited for Pete to join us after work. In the early evening Pete and I said good night to James and went to the tube at Warren Street. When we got there, there was a placard outside the station with a notice: 'Due to a body under a train at Highbury and Islington station, the Victoria line is closed between …' I didn't catch the rest, just thinking, well, good job that hasn't affected us – Highbury's on the Victoria line, but to get to Arsenal on the Piccadilly we change at King's Cross.

Mum and Doug.

Me and Sophie with our dad in his back garden in Stevenage – the family was celebrating a cousin's Holy Communion.

Sister act – the Slater girls hit Albert Square. That's (left to right) me as Lynne, Kacey Ainsworth as Little Mo, Michelle Ryan as Zoe, and Jessie Wallace as Kat.

One story involved us going to a fancy dress party – Kat, Big Mo (Laila Morse), Little Mo and me, flanked by dad Charlie (Derek Martin) and my boyfriend Garry (Ricky Groves). Must say I fancy myself with the flowing blonde locks.

Not a TV marriage made in heaven – Lynne and Garry finally tie the knot.

The Slaters with other EastEnders outside the Queen Vic.

A helping hand from Mum for me and my broken ankle. I seem to be looking at the pap who took this, but had no idea he was there.

The pap was visible this time – 'I can see you!' Big smile from me, newly pregnant and full of the joys of spring.

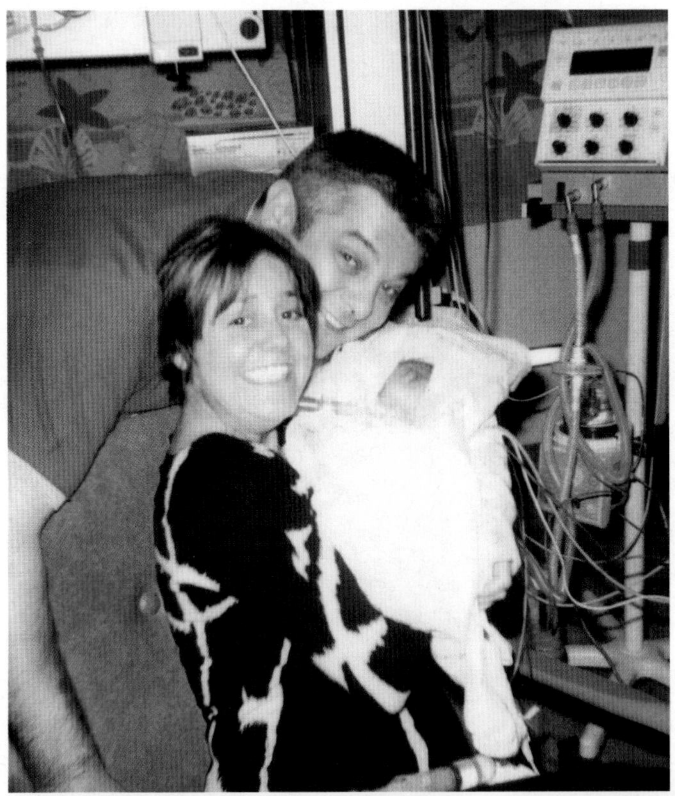

Our best Christmas present ever – the first time Pete and I could hold James. Tonny took the picture on Christmas Eve.

Mum holding James.

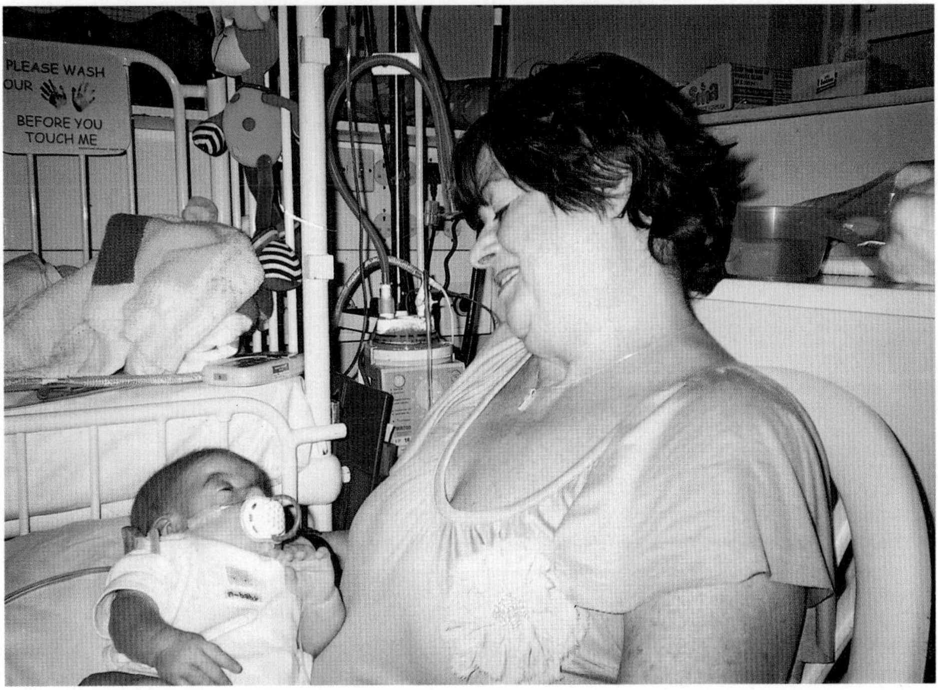

Me and Pete taking James on his first trip to the park – his first time out of hospital, in fact.

Mother love.

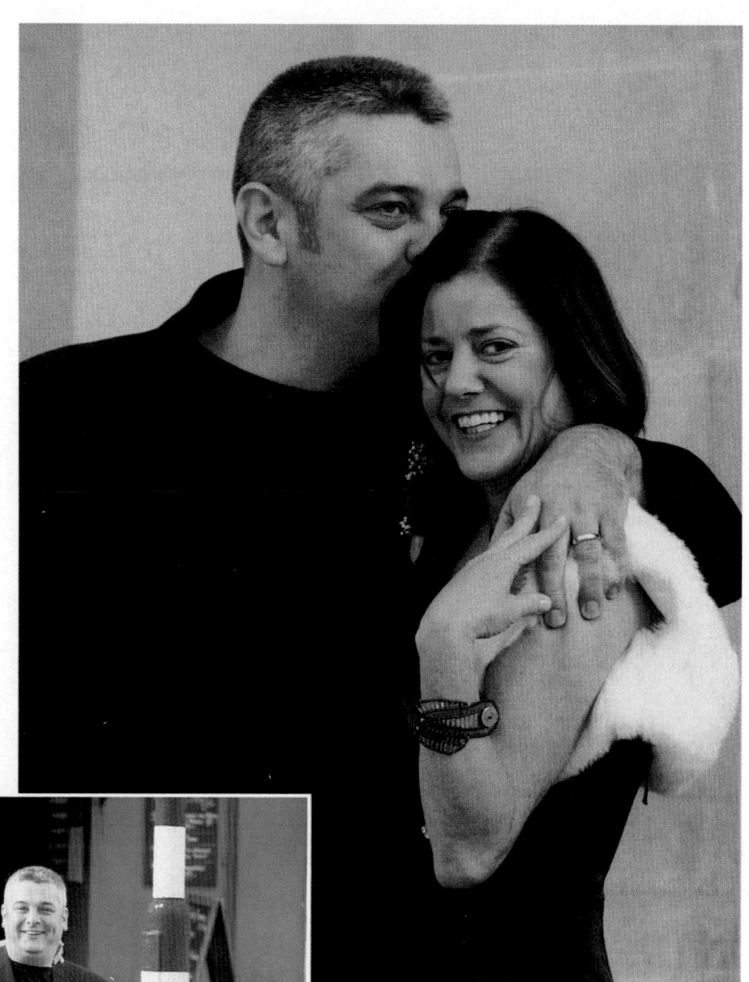

My real-life wedding – the happiest day of our lives.

Celebrating James's first birthday – you can see he's got his eye on those balloons.

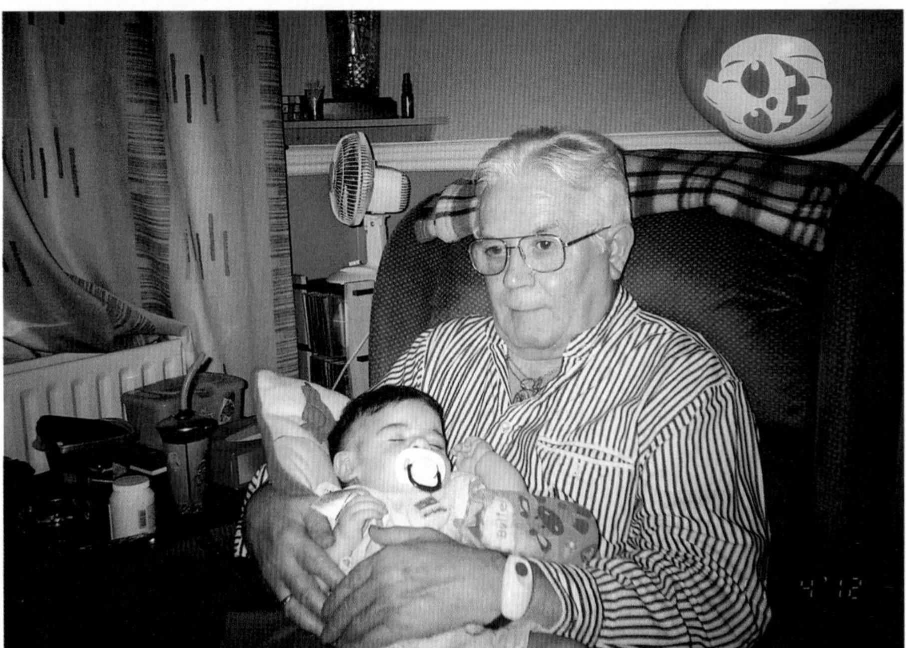

Asleep and content in Grandad's arms.

We got home and were thinking about dinner when Sophie phoned from Mum's flat.

'I tried to get hold of Mum at the crisis centre,' she told us. 'They said she'd left there about 12.30, and she hasn't returned. Nobody knows where she is.'

Oh God, we'd better start looking for her. Pete and I went out and checked local pubs. She wasn't in any of them, and nobody had seen her. Right, perhaps she's gone walk-about. Pete drove slowly all round the local streets, with me peering out at everyone and everything. No sign. Then we were driving up and down Highbury Fields – and I saw a figure huddled on a bench. It was dark by now, but I could just make out this figure.

'Stop the car!' I yelled at Pete. 'There she is!'

I leaped out of the car and ran over the grass to the bench. 'Mum!' I cried. 'Where the hell have you been all day?'

A startled face looked up at me – it was a stranger. Oh, for God's sake.

I got back in the car. I seriously had the hump with my mum now. 'Where the hell are you?' I said out loud. 'Don't torment us like this!'

Then I went cold. I saw again the board outside Warren Street station. I hadn't noticed if it had said the body was male or female. Could it ... 'Let's go back home,' I said to Pete. 'I wanna make a phone call.'

I rang the British Transport police and asked about the incident. They were cagey, not giving anything away – and I couldn't see why. Surely they wanted to know who the person was? Or, as I devoutly hoped, eliminate my mum from the inquiry. Then again, they probably have all sorts of strange people ringing up.

'Could you at least tell me if the body was male or female?' I asked them.

A female.

'How old?' I asked.

Between thirty and forty.

Thank God – that lets Mum out, then. Though she looked good for her age, she was in her early sixties.

I phoned Sophie with the news. She wasn't so easily reassured, and rang the police herself. She must have been more persuasive, because she got them to describe the clothes the person was wearing.

Next thing she's ringing at our doorbell. 'They said she was wearing Puma trainers with pink soles and grey tracksuit bottoms – I got her those! It's Mum!'

We sat frozen. Lots of other people have those clothes, surely? They're not uncommon.

Another ring at the bell. Sophie had given the police our address, and two officers were at the door. One of them was carrying a clear plastic bag with some objects in it. As soon as he walked in the door, I saw a bracelet inside the bag. A magnetic bracelet to stop arthritis pain. I'd given one just like it to Mum. There was a key – 'It's the key to the crisis centre,' said Sophie. Her voice was dull. A hammering filled my head and I couldn't breathe. Oh no oh no oh no – please no …

The policeman was speaking. He was very kind. He was saying something about the woman not dying immediately after she fell in front of the tube train. She'd been airlifted by helicopter to Whitechapel Hospital and the doctors had done everything they could for two hours before she'd finally slipped away. She had felt no pain, he said ...

No pain? Part of my mind was thinking, is that possible? Then he was saying, 'Someone has to come and identify the body.'

Oh my God, I couldn't.

'I'll go,' said Pete firmly. Always the rock. He left with the policeman.

Sophie and I sat in the living room. Someone, I don't know who, had rung Maureen, my mum's best friend, who still lived just up the road, and she came in with Debbie. My old friend Julie came in too. We all sat together.

Please don't let it be my mum, please don't let it be my mum. I don't wish death on anyone else, but please don't let it be my mum.

After an age Pete came back in. He held my hands, looked into my eyes and spoke quietly. 'It is Bernie.'

'No! No, please, Pete – is there any way it couldn't be Mum, someone who looks like her, is there any chance, any chance at all?'

'I'm so sorry,' he said.

'I've got to see her,' said Sophie with some force. 'I've got to be sure.'

Pete drove her to the hospital. I stayed sitting with

Maureen and Julie. I hardly dared breathe. Perhaps there was some hope left. Sophie had earlier phoned Dad, and Eileen brought him down from Stevenage.

The day was breaking when Pete brought Sophie back. She was white as a sheet. She'd collapsed.

Then the front door closed and there was just wailing.

*

The endless questions to someone who can't hear you and never will again. Why, Mum? Why did you do it? Did you mean to do it? Was it an accident? You were on the right platform to go to Warren Street, to the hospital, and the ticket in your pocket was the right price – were you going to see James? Did you feel dizzy, from the new tablets you were taking, and lose your balance? Or did something rise up in your heart and mind and make you think your life wasn't worth living? You meant to end it? How could you leave all the people who love you so much? When it was too late, when you'd started to fall, was there an instant you regretted it but it was too late?

And the accusations. How dare you! How dare you! You shouldn't have done this, you could have worked things out, had lots more years. Been happy again. You've left us! You've done us wrong! You've given us such pain! You were selfish – you, of all people!

And the images in the mind. The moment of impact – oh Mum, when I close my eyes I imagine that impact. It haunts me – the pain, the terror.

Then everything dissolves and there's just wave after battering wave of hurt. My mum's dead and I want her back.

*

What happened next is still a blur to me. I can't sort out the time. I do know that I went to see James as usual that Friday – Good Friday, as it happens. I knew I couldn't miss a day, as James would wonder where I was. And I suppose it was good to have something to do. So I got ready. I couldn't stop shaking – I had to force my arms into the sleeves of my jacket. Pete drove us there. The roads were quiet as it was a bank holiday.

I gave James a kiss and a cuddle and said hello, then sat there like a zombie. I couldn't be much use to him, so I didn't stay as long as usual.

There was the funeral to organize and people to tell. Dad was devastated. Despite his illness, he wanted to come to the funeral, with Eileen's help. He even went to see Mum lying in the chapel, and so did Aunty Mary – that's something I could never do. I want to remember Mum as she was in life. I can't bear to think of her any other way. I'd seen dead bodies, when relatives had died and you were expected to view them in the coffin. You had to touch their forehead and I hated it. So cold, so – not there. I didn't want the last time I saw Mum to be like that.

Dad came with Sophie, Pete and me to the funeral directors, and our cousin Kevin came too. We were using Miller's, who were wonderful, took everything out of our hands. Just as well, as there was a lot to do. Mum would first have a service in the local church, but then she'd go home – to her first home. She'd be buried in Enniskeane. The undertaker asked for Mum's full name, and then followed a surreal conversation.

'Julia Bernadette Lordan,' said Dad.

'No, Dad,' protested me and Sophie, 'you've got it wrong – it's Bernadette Julia.'

We thought he was losing the plot, to be honest. In the event, her headstone gives her first name as Bernadette, but we did find out later that it was really Julia. I don't know why both my parents used their middle names instead of their first names.

After the death I dragged myself through the days. Seeing James and thinking about the funeral made me focus on everyday things. Washing, dressing ... eating felt impossible, though, my throat was closed up. That's where my old mate Kathy came over all Irish on me – well, she would, as her parents are Irish, too. She's a brilliant cook and she made me lots of beautiful vegetable soup (she's a veggie), easy to digest. So when the hunger did kick in, I could manage the soup without too much trouble.

Mum's memorial service would be in Highbury, in the church of St Joan of Arc. She always liked things done nicely, so we did it by the book. A group of us, family and friends, the closest people, assembled in Mum's old flat in Matthews Court. We waited for the hearse to draw up outside, and got into the cars behind it. Dad followed the coffin in his motorized chair. We'd asked for the hearse to be 'walked' – the funeral director pacing slowly, with dignity, in front of it for the short journey to the church. Mum was saying goodbye to all the old familiar places – let her last journey here be slow.

We'd said no flowers, as the coffin was going to Ireland, but we'd asked for white lilies to be placed on top.

We drew up at the church, and went inside – and found the place packed out! Hundreds and hundreds of people had come to pay their respects, local people, friends Mum probably never knew she had. She was held in such respect and affection. People were having to stand at the back. We were so touched.

We took our places in the pews, and the coffin was brought in. Pete, Doug and cousin Kev were pallbearers, along with one of the men from Miller's. They walked slowly, carefully, the coffin steady on their shoulders. They placed it on the trestle. Beside it was a special tribute from Mum's best mate Maureen. She'd made a wonderful wreath of silk flowers, which framed a big colour photo of Mum, looking her most beautiful.

The service was conducted by Father Willy, our marvellous local priest. It was everything we'd hoped it would be. It did Mum justice. Then we held the wake, at the Highbury Barn pub – one of many where Mum had been so popular as a barmaid.

The next day, a Friday, Pete and I had to leave James for the first time. We'd be away in Ireland for three full days, so we arranged for friends to stand in for us. Our wonderful friends Julie, Kathy, Tilly and Tonny dropped everything to rally round. They would tend James with as much love and tenderness as Pete and I would, especially giving him his bath, which he loved. Dad was determined to go to Ireland, too, despite his debilitating illness. Pete and Kevin were an enormous support to him.

So all of us, close family and friends, flew to Cork. I tried not to think of the coffin, travelling with us as cargo. I was trying to hold myself together, though to tell the truth I was in pieces.

At Cork airport, the coffin was treated with dignity. It was carried off the plane, and an Irish flag was draped over it. Pallbearers carried it to the hearse, and we all took our places in the following cars. We arrived at the funeral home in Enniskeane and left the coffin there until the morning. We wished Mum good night.

Next day, we sat in the funeral home next to the coffin, in ranks of chairs – almost as if it was a wedding. Eileen hadn't come over with Dad, so Pete and Kevin had made sure that he was as smartly dressed as he always was, even shaving him – and Dad wouldn't let just anyone do that. People from all around, friends and relations, came up to us and shook hands. 'Sorry for your trouble …' 'Sorry for your trouble …' Mum had been as well loved here, in her old home, as she was in London.

The parish church was just a two-minute walk away, so Sophie and I thought it would be respectful to walk behind the hearse. Mum was going to be buried in the churchyard with her brother Jerry, the handsome charmer who died too young. Poor Uncle DP, who'd been so cruelly crippled by arthritis, had died by now, too, and he'd been buried in the same churchyard, with their parents.

It was a fine spring day, the sun was shining. Sophie had brought a lot of red roses, and she gave them to the people closest to Mum. We all stood around the graveside, while the service was read. It was as touching as the first. Once more the coffin had been carried by Pete, Doug and Kev, this time helped by Derry, one of our Irish cousins. Now they lowered it into the ground. We threw our red roses on top of it. I looked away for only an instant, and when I looked back there was a dark cover over the coffin, with a silver cross on it. Mum was gone.

We went back to Mahoney's, a pub down the road, for the wake. There was good food (well, there would have to be – Mum was such a good cook!) and plenty of drink. A constant murmur of 'Sorry for your trouble ...'

Well, Mum, we did our best. We wanted to show how much we loved you, and the day did go well. Only two things weren't in keeping. Maureen left her lovely wreath by the graveside – and someone nicked it. And while I was walking behind the hearse, photographers snapped me with a long lens, so next day's *Irish Sun* could print my picture on the front page and show its readers 'Elaine's grief'. I hope it choked them.

*

We flew back to London on the Tuesday, after a couple of days seeing people and sorting things out. The formalities were over. But I couldn't grieve properly for my mum. There were all those bloody questions. I've thought and thought, backwards and forwards, inside and out, gone over all the details.

Nothing will bring her back, of course – if wishing could make it so, she'd be beside me right now. But it's just so hard. Losing someone you love is bad enough, but suicide? It makes everything so mixed up. Would I feel the same if, God forbid, Mum had had a fatal illness and died naturally? No, I would not. I could accept that, in time.

Sophie had told me about the last time she'd seen Mum. It was the day before she died, the Wednesday, in the crisis centre.

'Mum was shaking,' she said. 'It was her new medication, it was making her legs shake. And she was totally exhausted – she hadn't slept for so long, and she was getting agitated. She was really down and I was really worried about her.'

Mum had been asking for something to help her sleep, but for some reason she didn't get it. So she was getting more and more exhausted.

Sophie went on, 'I rang the centre the next day and spoke to Mum. I said I'd come and see her, but she knew I was applying for a new course and told me to go and do that first. So I said I'd drop round later. That was the last time I spoke to her.'

Sophie got to the centre about 12.30, but Mum had gone out – to the shops, a member of staff said. She'd only be a few minutes. Sophie sat and waited, of course in vain. Then the nightmare unfolded.

We've talked all round this, Sophie and me. Mum just hadn't been getting the help she needed to get to sleep. If only she'd had some respite, she could have recovered her strength. If she'd had better treatment, she would never have done what she did. How could she think straight, in her condition?

She must have decided to go and see James, and when she was on the platform and saw the train coming, something was triggered in her brain. She must have been in torment, and thought she could make the pain stop.

But it's my firm belief, and Sophie's, that Mum did not intend to kill herself. She would be alive today if only she'd had better medication. With proper rest and recuperation, she could have been her old self again. And we would still have our mum.

I couldn't help thinking how ironic it was. My baby was having the best possible treatment on the NHS, the best skills and techniques freely available, with the best possible dedicated staff. How come another part of the Health Service failed my mum? We all know that mental health is the Cinderella of medicine – but why? When the consequences can be just as terrible as any physical disease. Is it really just a matter of money, or is the political will not there?

After all, as my mum might have said, no one ignores you

when you have a broken leg, so why do you become invisible when it's your mind that's broken?

*

Later, when Sophie and I were sorting through Mum's things, we found a note she'd written. We think it was something the crisis centre asked her to do when she first went there, to describe how she felt, because it was headed 'Depression'. She mentioned Sophie, James, me and Pete, how she worried for us, and how much Doug had meant to her. As for herself, she wrote, 'Fear of future. I feel I'm in a wilderness. I never thought I'd reach the circumstances I'm in right now, I thought that only happened to other people. How wrong I was.'

Surely there could have been a way out of the wilderness for her?

CHAPTER NINE

Home at Last

It's like putting your emotions on hold. I couldn't go to pieces after Mum's death, I had to keep a tight control. I forced myself to do what I had to do, pushing the terrible reality into some place in my mind, where it would stay – at least during the day, when I had to be busy. The night was a different matter. Every time I shut my eyes, I'd picture that awful moment, the moment when the train hit Mum – everything in me flinched from it, but still it kept crowding into my mind.

Of course I had to concentrate on James, I wanted to do my best for him. Over the last three months, I'd been learning how to carry out the special procedures to help him breathe and eat. I had to get pitch perfect in these – when he came home we wouldn't have the dedicated hospital staff on hand to help. Pete had been learning all the procedures, too, but he'd be out at work for a lot of the day and I'd be by myself. We had to be alert to James's condition all the time.

There'd been another scare when Pete and I were in Ireland for Mum's funeral – in fact at one point we thought we were going to have to fly back early. The first convenient flight back was on the following Tuesday morning, and we had planned to spend Sunday and Monday seeing people, sorting out the paperwork, all that kind of thing. Meanwhile we phoned the hospital every day in the morning, afternoon and evening to get an update on James. He seemed stable. Then before we could phone on the Sunday evening, I had a call on my mobile. James had been taken back to intensive care – another emergency. Fluid had got onto his lungs, which was very dangerous for him. Healthy people can just cough it up, but James's lungs weren't sufficiently developed yet to do that. We'd already learned just how quickly his condition could change – one moment he'd be fine, then the next he wasn't.

'Should we come back right away?' we asked. Yes, you'd better, was the reply.

So Pete spent hours on the phone desperately trying to book a flight. There was no internet access where we were staying, but in any case, if you're trying to organize something in a hurry, a Sunday night isn't the best time to be doing it. As it happened, before we'd managed to find a flight, the hospital phoned back, telling us that James had stabilized, thank God. When we phoned again later that evening, they said, 'Don't worry. He's a lot better now – you don't have to dash back.'

We said to each other that that was James's little shout to us – 'I'm still here! Where are you?'

When we arrived home, we went straight to James to tell him we were back. Then life quickly settled back into the routine we'd got used to – going to the hospital every day, helping with James's care. The good news was that he was improving, generally getting stronger. At last there seemed to be a light at the end of the tunnel. He was gradually moved into what's called special care, as opposed to intensive care. It's like moving to the bed nearest the door in a hospital ward as you gradually get better – then you're out of there!

James came out of special care in June, and was transferred to Galaxy Ward in UCLH for a couple of weeks. And then Pete and I heard the words we'd been longing for. James was six months and one week, and after endless tests and consultations and procedures, the doctors told us, 'You can take your baby home.'

*

We were over the moon, but also very aware of the huge responsibility that was now on us. We asked the doctors from the neonatal unit what was the first thing we should do to prepare for James's homecoming. Their answer took us by surprise.

'Take a break.'

What? With everything to arrange, the flat to get ready, the equipment to sort out …

'You need a break,' they said. 'The last time you were away from your son, that was hardly a rest. Have some time to yourselves, as a couple. Recharge your batteries.'

As they told us, 'You're going to need all your energy.'

Well, these were the oddest doctor's orders I've ever been

given, but Pete and I duly arranged for friends to stand in for us. As well as the usual suspects – Sophie, Julie, Tonny, Kathy and Tillie – my old friends Jane and Wizz took our place in the hospital, and did a great job. As ever, it was such a relief that we could depend on good friends to help us out. For our break we had a long weekend in Nice. Which was nice. We'd been there before, when I was pregnant, and had liked it a lot. This time we did have a good rest, phoning the hospital a couple of times a day to check on James.

When we got back, it was time for Operation Getting James Home – well, it felt like a military manoeuvre with all the organization involved. Two or three days before James was due to leave hospital, we had an oxygenator machine delivered. This was about the size of a small fridge, and we parked it in the hall, plugged into a handy electric socket. It made a low-level humming noise, which we got used to after a while. This machine generates oxygen out of the air, and supplies it wherever it's needed – James would need it in the bedroom, the kitchen and the living room. So plastic tubing snaked from the machine all over the place. Pete hit on the ingenious idea of feeding it out of windows and back in again, to cut down on trailing clutter inside (being plastic, it was weatherproof).

Very sensibly, there was a back-up oxygen supply in case of a power cut – in which case the oxygenator would sound an alarm. We stored this back-up in the wardrobe, the only piece of furniture big enough to take it. It was a huge oxygen cylinder, taller than me, which weighed a ton and came with all sorts of screws and valves and dials and special tools for turning it on and off. We were also given smaller – thankfully much smaller – versions of this, portable cylinders, like little fire extinguishers. One of these would fit under James's pram when we took him out. We used to get the cylinders on prescription from the local chemist's. We'd take along an empty cylinder, and exchange it for a full one – brings a whole new meaning to taking back the empties!

Incidentally, going back to the oxygenator machine in the hall – it was always plugged in, and we simply assumed that the cost would be included in our electricity bill (that's if we thought about it at all, which we probably didn't). To our surprise, though, we got a refund. The machine has its own meter, and works out how much electricity it uses, so you don't have to pay for it. And this without the bureaucratic fuss of filling in forms and stating your income and so on. A small example of NHS joined-up thinking, perhaps, but it shows that somebody's actually worked out even this implication for families on a tight budget, and made it an automatic payment.

Other equipment ... we were also supplied with a monitor to check the oxygen saturation in James's blood (always called 'sats'). We'd got used to using this machine in hospital – it's quite a compact piece of kit, about the size of a large shoebox, with a digital display on the front. You just clip a red-light-emitting diode onto a toe or finger, and it shines through, measuring the oxygen level. Don't ask me how it works – I'm just glad it's a non-invasive procedure for a change, with no more heel-pricks.

So there we were, all set up to welcome James home. We'd placed his cot in our bedroom – he always had to be close by – and fortunately there was plenty of space. It's a big airy room, so we didn't have to squeeze him and his equipment into a corner.

On that first night back from the hospital, when we saw him lying peacefully in his own cot, we could have cried. At last he was home with us.

*

So began another new way of life. We'd learned how to look after James in the hospital, and now we were doing it at home. Thank God we'd had all that training, all that practice – the responsibility is huge. But you really do get used to it, you learn to take it in your stride.

At first James was on oxygen 24/7, with an oxygen tube attached to the end of his cannula (that's the thin tubes going into his nostrils, attached to his cheeks by pieces of tape). That little piece of equipment was another thing we had to keep an eye on, as it can get clogged, so we had a store of spares and changed it every day or so. We monitored his sats regularly and adjusted the oxygen flow accordingly. As long as the sats read 95 or 96 per cent, that was OK, but if they dropped, then we had to increase the oxygen by a precise amount. Everything was carefully metered – we had to know precisely how much to give him at any time, obviously in consultation with the community nurses (more about them later). Not that we ever had to give him enormous amounts – compared to other babies in his situation he usually needed relatively little, more like a top-up.

It was the same with feeding, and giving him his medicines – carefully measured amounts. We'd measure out his formula into what looked like syringes without the needles – we always had a stockpile of syringes, so to anyone who didn't know us, the flat must have looked like junkie heaven! Then this was plugged into the end of the feeding tube that led into James's stomach – you just held up the container and let gravity do the work.

James was still suffering with reflux. The Nissen fundoplication procedure he'd had in April to ease it had worked only for a while, which isn't uncommon, apparently. He'd be fed through the tube, and keep the food down and we'd think, fantastic! Then he'd have another meal four hours later, which would also stay down – even more fantastic! Then up would come everything. Very distressing all round. He was put on the list for a repeat operation, but meanwhile the sound of the washing machine was almost as incessant as the oxygenator in the hall.

Sometimes he had a reflux attack in the middle of a feed, and the stuff would come bubbling back up the tube. Once he'd finished a feed, you had to be very careful not to disturb him for a good while. He had to be quite still, to give his stomach the best chance of digesting his food. This could lead to a dilemma when he happened to have filled his nappy at the same time – change him and risk more reflux, or leave him undisturbed but uncomfortable? Tricky.

Not that he complained much, far from it. Considering what he'd been through, he was such an easy baby. He hardly ever cried – only when he was uncomfortable, which was usually from the reflux. And if we overslept in the morning and were a bit late with his feed, he wouldn't be yelling for it – just lying there gurgling to himself, perfectly alert, moving his eyes to look round the room. I have a feeling – and I don't know if this could be scientifically backed up – that when babies have experienced a lot of pain, one way or another, it makes them more resistant to lesser discomforts.

With his reflux problem, it was a wonder James had managed to fill out at all, but he was gorgeous, positively cuddly, not a bit scraggy. So he must have been keeping down just enough of the formula.

We timed our lives by James's feeds – regular as clockwork (well, almost). First, 8 a.m., then midday, then 4 p.m., then 8 p.m, and finally midnight. We'd put him to bed after the 8 p.m. feed – always lying on his back, slightly raised – and he'd be asleep long before midnight. Then, for his last feed, we'd have to be very careful and quiet not to wake him if we wanted to go straight to bed ourselves. We noticed that this final feed always went down (literally) more successfully than the others, and he'd usually sleep through. Perhaps he was more relaxed, I don't know, or maybe he was like his mum and just liked his kip! But it was very reassuring, and we started to put just a little extra in that feed to make up for any lost later on. After all, he would have eight hours to digest it, rather than four. Not that we ever overloaded him, of course – everything was always a matter of the right balance.

We gave him his medicines in the same way as his feeds, using very small syringes as the amounts were so tiny, sometimes just 0.5ml. We'd have to help gravity along, pushing the plunger. He had meds for his reflux, and also something to thin the blood, which would ease pressure on his heart. One of his meds was called Domperidone – when I first heard it mentioned in the hospital I thought, 'Dom Perignon? He's a bit young for champagne, isn't he?'

In case you're thinking that this routine must have felt like relentless drudgery for us, it wasn't. True, we had to be extra vigilant, and there was more work involved in feeding him than with a healthy baby, but we were only doing what any parents would do for their baby. We loved him, we wanted to do the best for him, give him every chance for a healthy life. Quite straightforward, really.

Pete and I had a huge advantage, though – because we were so close, we were of one mind when it came to looking after James, it came naturally. Long before he was born, we knew our relationship was rock solid. The demands of looking after a poorly child can drive some couples apart, and what a tragedy that is. But we were fortunate – we always knew that the extra responsibility we had with our son would never come between us.

What's more, we had the best professional support network you could wish for – joined-up thinking on a grand scale. Whenever people gripe about paying taxes, I always say, 'You wouldn't say that if you saw how people in the NHS work.' Quite simply, the medical people we met were stars. In the hospital, every member of staff, from consultant to junior nurse, was doing their job, what they're paid for, sure, but without exception they went further than that. To Pete and me they were really kind, thoughtful and made a difficult experience more tolerable. We built up a strong, trusting relationship. As for James, they were so tender-hearted, so loving. Talk about going the extra mile – you can't put that on a balance sheet!

And now that James was home, we were finding that this level of care continued. In normal circumstances, you'd take a healthy baby to the clinic to get weighed and so on, but with James, a lot of the care came to him. Community nurses visited regularly. They weighed James every week, being careful to use the same scales as his weight was a critical factor in his condition. I remember one disconcerting occasion when he managed to poo into the scales – though come to think of it, wouldn't he weigh the same whether it was in or out? Passing quickly on …

The nurses also checked James's sats, of course. They were optimistic about his oxygen needs, and I remember at least one nurse saying, 'We'll get him off oxygen in no time.' Every week or so we'd do an overnight study, leaving James hooked up to the monitor all night to see how his levels fluctuated, and the nurse would take the machine back next morning to read the results. We might be told, 'In the middle of the night his levels tend to drop – oxygen does drop when they're asleep – so put the amount up to 200ml.' But, as I say, he usually needed only relatively small amounts.

James also came under the care of the local Child Development Team. He'd been mostly lying in a cot for six months, so naturally he was behind with his development. He'd never been able to even try to crawl as the feeding tube stopped him lying on his front, and the tube could be uncomfortable – he'd pulled it out more than once. Eventually he was fitted with a neat little button to close off the feeding tube. When Pete first saw it, he said, 'That looks like the little valve you put in a beach ball!' It was a great improvement, and meant he was finally ready for a kind of baby workout.

The Child Development Team is dedicated to bringing a child up to the stage he should be at for his age. A team of three or four people visited regularly, primarily the physiotherapist, who devised little exercises for James, and taught us how to work with him. We'd do things like sit him on our laps, holding his hands and letting him pull himself forward. Again, timing was crucial for exercising – because of the reflux, it had to be about half an hour *before* a feed.

There was also a speech and language therapist, whose title I found confusing. Speech and language? In a six-month-old? Would they be teaching him French? He'd know more than me, then, I thought. I quickly realized that the therapist's job was all about James's mouth and tongue, which at this stage meant feeding techniques.

The long-term goal, needless to say, was for James to eat normally, taking food into his mouth and swallowing, at which point the feeding tube could be closed off. Babies who are fed through a tube often develop an aversion to having anything in their mouths, but fortunately James loved his dummy – that was a really good sign in a baby who'd never been orally fed. That got him used to the sensation of having something in his mouth. Meanwhile, we had to encourage him to develop a swallowing action. We'd smear puréed food around his mouth to get him used to taste and texture as he licked his lips. We started him off with sweet things – he loved apple purée. And we'd introduce tiny drops of water, really tiny, very carefully. There was the ever-present danger of getting fluid on his lungs, which he wouldn't be able to cough up.

Some of the development team worked in the hospital, so we'd take James to their clinics. His eyesight and hearing were checked, and both were fine.

As well as all these people helping James to fulfil his potential in every way, there was care for me too – the respite nurse would come along and I'd have time off, four hours a week in all, which I could use as I liked. I usually went over to my sister Sophie's and had a kip. Or, if we were feeling up to it, we'd go to Mum's flat in Matthews Court and get on with sorting out her things.

I can't speak too highly of all the people we became involved with, the nurses and therapists and other specialists. They came into our life and became part of it. They did their jobs to the highest professional standards, while on a personal level they were delightful – warm and good-humoured, people you'd always want to be friends with. James wasn't just a patient to them, they interacted with him, talked to him, laughed with him, had a real emotional bond.

So you're not on your own! What's more, as well as the medical people, we'd always been blessed with the help and support of our friends. They'd stood in for us at the hospital, tending James with all the love and care you could hope for. I'd thought that when James was home and Pete was working, I'd mostly be by myself, but friends were always popping round and offering help. The children, too. Pete's kids had been so sweet to James in hospital – now, when they visited, they competed to mix up James's feed and pour it into the tube, and they knew all about making sure he was in the correct position to take his feed – sitting upright and supported. James's big sister learned to prepare all his meds, too, and laid them out ready. All this was under close supervision, I hasten to add.

My friend Julie's daughter Ellie often used to visit at the same time as Pete's kids, and she was particularly devoted to James. In fact, Julie told me that after Ellie first saw James, she went home and put away all her dolls and soft toys.

'What are you doing that for?' Julie asked her.

'I've got a real baby to look after now,' was the reply.

These children – they were so careful, so meticulous, so conscientious. It was as if this little baby, needing so much help, brought out a nurturing side that you wouldn't normally notice in lively, noisy kids racketing all over the place.

*

We'd take James out for walks in his pushchair to get some fresh air. We had to take him to different clinics, including the chronic lung clinic and the heart clinic. He needed an operation on his heart. As well as the lungs, the pressure had affected his heart, literally shunting it from the left side to the right. Amazingly, James's heart had pulled itself back into the correct position, but obviously this had caused some stress and strain, and there'd been a small tear in some tissue, which was stopping the heart pumping blood round efficiently.

The procedure to correct it is absolutely incredible. It's done as a day case. A line is put into one of the major arteries in the leg, and pushed all the way up into the heart, where it puts a tiny cork in the tear to block it. We were just waiting for James to put on more weight before he could have this operation.

In the event, though, it wasn't to be.

*

It was while we were taking James to one of his clinics that the outside world broke in on me. My whole life was revolving round James, with the daily routine of feeding, cleaning, monitoring, changing – and playing. I used to sing and talk to him, tickle and stroke him, and he'd smile and kick his legs. He was already showing signs of a real little personality, and he was adorable. The world outside the flat and the hospital hardly existed for me.

The clinic was in Great Ormond Street this time, a few weeks after James came home. We had an appointment with Professor Piero, about James's reflux problem. Pete was driving, but he had to go on to work that morning, so my cousin Kevin, who was staying with us, offered to accompany me and James into the hospital.

So there we were driving along in the car, Pete and Kev in front, me in the back with James and all his gear, including his pushchair and one of the little portable oxygen cylinders that fitted underneath it. Suddenly we heard a whole load of sirens going off, while masses of police cars, ambulances and fire engines were zooming up and down the roads. What the hell was going on? Pete turned on the radio, and we heard that there'd been a disturbance on the tube, a power surge. Obviously there was going to be all kinds of chaos and traffic jams.

Now the police were everywhere, telling everybody driving or walking, 'Move along, move along.' Pete was worried about being late for work and I was worried about missing James's appointment. I said, 'I've got James's pushchair – why don't me and Kev just get out and walk?'

Pete knows London very well, and he's good at finding all kinds of alternative routes. He said, 'I'll try just one more way round.' He doubled back, and cut around the south side of Tavistock Square. If he hadn't, James, Kev and me would have got out and been walking past the bus in the square just as it exploded.

It was the 7th of July, and this was the Number 30 bus that was blown up by a suicide bomber. As it happened, while we saw the explosion and were engulfed in the clouds of smoke, Pete was able to drive us safely away from it.

Absolute shock. I was immediately in a real panic, thinking, 'Explosion – fire – oxygen cylinder – inflammable!' All I could think about was getting away from the bus and getting James and his oxygen cylinder away from the fire. I was starting to hyperventilate, and Kev broke in with, 'For God's sake, I'm gonna need some of James's oxygen meself in a minute.' He phoned his boyfriend Andrew, who said the trouble was from power surges on the tube, so Kev said, 'No, it's not power surges, it's bombs, bloody bombs! They're everywhere!'

We could have no idea at the time just how devastating the bombs were, how many people would be killed and terribly injured going about their ordinary business, how many lives would be changed for ever. We were just thinking of getting away from danger, and getting to where we needed to go. Somehow Pete managed to find a way through to the hospital, running red lights, avoiding road-blocks. And I have to say the police were really brave – we could see them running past us, in the direction of the bomb, telling people to move along and pulling people off buses ... everything in a state of confusion, nobody knowing when and where another bomb might go off.

We reached the hospital at last – and it was surreal. Here the streets were abnormally quiet and empty. We parked right outside the hospital, where usually there are no free spaces at all. We all went inside, Pete as well. He couldn't have driven to work, not that he would have left us anyway now. We told the reception staff what had happened. This was so soon after the blast that news hadn't reached them yet, and they were really upset, in tears – 'Oh my God, what's happening?' Like most people in the city that day, they were immediately worried about friends and colleagues.

At first, it was business as usual. We went down to the clinic in the basement area and were seen straight away. So far, not many people had turned up, and we could only hope that other patients and medical people hadn't been caught up in the bombing. After that, we went upstairs to make phone calls on the land lines, knowing that you shouldn't use mobiles in hospitals, but not realizing that the mobile network was out of action anyway. Then we had to go downstairs again – in fact everybody was ushered out of the main reception area. We gathered that the hospital was taking adult casualties, which is unusual for Great Ormond Street – there'd been another blast nearby, in Russell Square tube station. The scale of the disaster was becoming horribly clear. The reception area was going to serve as an emergency treatment centre – there were even beds in the covered walkway outside.

The hospital staff looked after us very well, laying on tea and coffee and sandwiches, and setting up a little portable telly so we could follow the news. Everyone was desperate to know what was going on, and clustered round the fuzzy images on the TV set, people taking it in turns to hold the aerial out of the window to improve reception. There was even a smoking area set up in a corner of the outside play area, and here Kev and I managed to get ourselves into trouble. I went out across the playground to have a cig, and met Kev coming back. So far, so good. On my way back, I meant to walk past a large model of a bus they've got there for the kids to play on – and cracked my head on a bit sticking out. When I got back to reception, there was Kev standing with a nurse, filling in an accident report.

'I cracked me head on the bloody bus,' he told me.

'So did I,' I said.

Then the nurse said, 'Oh, you should fill in a report too.'

'I don't need to do that,' I said, 'it's nothing.'

But she insisted. As I said to Kev, imagine what the admin people will think when they get two reports of identical accidents, one for Kevin Lordan and one for Elaine Lordan. Those Lordans must be a right lot, can't avoid a stationary model bus when it's in front of them.

This is a silly story, I know, and so inconsequential when you think what was happening that day. I only mention it because I've noticed that daft things often happen in the middle of really bad things. It reminds me of the time me and Mum got the giggles when we saw the dog attacking its reflection in a puddle – even though we were feeling awful after leaving my sister Sophie at Friern Barnet Hospital. And

Pete witnessed something totally incongruous when he went to identify my mum's body in Whitechapel Hospital. The two policemen he was with didn't know the hospital any more than he did, so they were all wandering around looking for the morgue. At one point a strange bloke staggered up to them and said, 'Do you know where the A&E is? I've really overdone it on the coke tonight.' Just the thing to tell the cops. And when Mum's identity was confirmed, after the British Transport policeman had told me the woman was between thirty and forty, it flashed through my mind how flattered she would have been that she looked much younger than her years!

Back in Great Ormond Street, we stayed most of the afternoon. It had been a long day. We managed to keep up James's routine, feeding and changing him, and that gave us a semblance of normality. Otherwise it was like being in a war zone – not that I've ever been in one, thank God, but that day we had a taste of what it must be like. Random violence, deaths, casualties lined up on trolleys – and the fear, the uncertainty. Then there's the other side of the coin, what other people are capable of. The medical staff were working ceaselessly under huge pressure, not knowing if their friends and colleagues were safe. And there was one hero in particular at the hospital. Pete got chatting to some medical staff, who told him about one of their doctors. He'd been on the tube train that had been blown up at Russell Square. He walked to the back of the train, got out through the door, and walked all the way back along the line to King's Cross. Then he went to the surface, and walked all through the streets to get to Great Ormond Street, and promptly started treating casualties, including those who'd been hurt in the train he'd been travelling in. What can you say?

We finally left the hospital at about five o'clock. All day, the police had ordered people to stay indoors, wherever they were, as nobody knew if another bomb was going to go off. But by this time, most people were getting restless, desperate to go home – I know we were. The police still weren't keen, but left it up to individuals to decide what to do. 'We'd prefer you to stay for your own safety,' they said, 'but if you really want to leave, then do.' So most of us did. The roads were still quiet, and there were loads of people just walking, walking, walking … Ours was about the only car on the road. It was so strange – empty roads yet so many people around.

Were we relieved to get home! As I was getting James ready for bed, I thought about how hard he'd fought to stay alive all these months, how precious his life was. Yet he could so easily have been caught up in the explosions earlier that day – in fact, we could all have been killed, along with other people completely unknown to the bomber. I just can't get my head round it.

*

James had his first holiday later that month. Pete's mum was longing to meet her latest grandchild, but wasn't really up to the journey herself. So we hired a people carrier and off we went to Yorkshire, with Pete's three children too. Before we planned the trip, James had been doing really well with his oxygen levels, but then they dipped a little and we had to up his intake. Of course we wondered whether we should take him on such a long journey, especially as we were driving down to Cornwall straight afterwards, and so we discussed it with the community nurses.

Why had the sats gone down? He was still suffering from reflux, but that shouldn't have affected his oxygen levels. We'd been hoping that the repeat Nissen fundoplication operation would have been done by now, but there had been delays. It was probably because of his heart problem – the heart and lungs being intimately linked, the damaged heart was probably having to work overtime to get the blood into his lungs. Then there was the fact that James was getting bigger, and more active – good things in themselves, but also putting more strain on his heart and lungs. We were advised that yes, we could take James away, but to be on the safe side we should keep him on low-level oxygen 24/7, until the repeat fundoplication.

So we felt confident enough to set off. Mind you, it was a trip and a half – more like another military operation. It took a couple of hours to load up the car with all of James's gear, including the all-important oxygenator, along with the portable cylinders and sats monitor. Not forgetting all his medical notes in case an emergency happened and we had to take him to a strange hospital. During the trip I sat in the front with Pete, who did all the driving, while his children were in the back with James. Pete's older daughter was a huge help, making up James's feeds and generally looking after him, but with her brother and sister also insisting on taking their turn.

We were staying with Pete's sister Cath and her husband Mike, who live in a big comfortable house in a North Yorkshire village with their four children, three girls and a boy, aged between nine and seventeen. Good job it's a big house – with Pete's mum there too, there'd be thirteen of us altogether. Millie was thrilled to see James and adored him on sight. For the first time all eight of her grandchildren were together, and she really made the most of it – loads of photos were taken of her holding James, with the older children grouped around her. James's medical paraphernalia – he was wearing the cannula all the time now – didn't faze her at all, while for Cath it would have been familiar as she used to be a nurse.

It wasn't long before we'd settled in and sorted out all James's stuff – Pete called it 'tubing up the house'. Then it was time for some fun. The weather was gorgeous and we had several excursions to Scarborough. We wheeled James on to the beach in his pushchair, oxygen cylinder stored underneath as usual, and watched everybody having a good time. James really seemed to enjoy his first sight of the seaside.

After the Yorkshire break, we'd planned to go to the other end of the country, to Cornwall. After my mum's death, lovely Steve McFadden had been really sympathetic. He owns a cottage in Cornwall and he'd said, 'If you want to get away, at any time, it's yours – stay as long as you like.' We were more than happy to take him up on his offer. We came back home from Yorkshire, unloaded everything, did the washing, loaded up again, and off we went to Cornwall next morning.

We were lucky with the weather again – it was warm and sunny, ideal for the seaside. Pete's children loved it, and James was turning into a bit of a beach bum, too. We also had the use of Steve's motorboat, quite a big one with a cabin and everything. We all went out in it, and James got his sea legs in no time – if you can have sea legs sitting in a pushchair. He loved it.

One day I had a chance to strike a blow for children's lib, so to speak. We were all on a family beach, and Pete's younger two were larking about and running around, as kids do. Apparently they'd annoyed an older couple on the beach, who told them to 'Sod off.' They were quite upset by this, so, as Pete was occupied feeding James behind a windbreak, I went over to the couple to sort it out.

'Did you tell my kids to sod off?' I asked them. I know they're my stepchildren, but I wasn't about to go into details.

'Well, they were making a lot of noise and kicking sand up as they ran by,' said the grumpy couple, who had West Country accents.

'Hello?' I said. 'Look over there – see the bouncy castle and the fairground? This is obviously a kids' beach. Kids play on it. Clearly you're from around here, so you must know where the secluded beaches are – so if you don't like it, why don't you sod off yourselves to one of those?'

Quite restrained, I thought.

Anyway, they got up and went soon after. It may have been trivial, but I was really annoyed – talk about children being seen and not heard. What a horrible attitude. You want them to run around and use up their energy in a playground, and that's what the beach there was.

Mind you, there were times that week when I was grateful for some peace and quiet myself. The cottage was in a beautiful, secluded spot, and now and then it was good to just soak up the tranquillity. I still wasn't letting myself go about Mum's death. It was always in my mind, of course, and I promised myself I would grieve properly later, when I didn't have so much going on. Meanwhile, I kept pushing everything down, including the awful prospect of the inquest, which still hadn't been arranged. It was the odd thing that would trigger me off, though. One day, a few weeks earlier, I'd been doing a bit more sorting through her old flat – what a business it is, sorting out people's things – and an envelope had slipped out of a book. Perhaps Mum had used it as a bookmark. There was a letter inside, and – I know you'll forgive me, Mum – I read it.

It nearly finished me off. It was from a young friend of hers, Joanna, a Polish student learning English in London, who had worked part-time in the same bar as Mum. I don't know exactly when it was written – there's no date on the letter and the postmark had been smudged. In the middle of her chatty, newsy letter, Joanna reminisced about her time in London:

> Every Wednesday, Thursday and Friday I was waiting till 12.00 (actually 12.15 because you were always late!) because after that time, work was just a pleasure. Why? Because Bernie was behind the bar and the Archway Tavern from 12.15 till 5 was taking heart. Archway without you was life without the soul! Yes! I'm not telling you that because I'm trying to be nice! I'm telling you that because it's a truth! Everyone loves you!!

Life without the soul … I think I know what she meant.

*

The double dose of sea air seemed to do James good. His cheeks looked pinker and he was more energetic, kicking his legs in his little chair. We'd bought the chair when he was still in hospital and he loved it. Talk about bells and whistles. It had a massage mechanism that soothed him, and all sorts of gizmos that made noises and turned lights on. James quickly learned how to work them all.

He still had to go back to hospital for regular tests, though, and I remember one time that summer when he asserted himself. He had to stay overnight and have his blood taken every two hours for twenty-four hours, while I stayed with him. It was difficult to get a line in – he'd had so many of them that his poor little veins were just about blown to bits. The nurses took it from his heel – a little prick, and then squeezing the blood out. All the time I'd be saying, 'It's all right, darling, Mummy's here, Mummy's here.'

Well, the next day I got him home – and he wouldn't look at me. Totally blanked me. Just turned his head. When Julie popped in, with a 'How are you then, darling?' he was all smiles. And when Pete came home from work, it was a big beautiful smile for him too. Obviously he blamed me for the tests – seven months old and he blanks me! It took him hours to come round and forgive me. Now I knew how my mum must have felt when I blanked her all those years ago.

In September he at last had his second Nissen fundoplication, and this time it seemed to take really well – his reflux was greatly reduced, and so was his need for oxygen. He usually needed it only at night now. Meanwhile, he was still having regular visits from the community nurses, the physio and all the other specialists. It was arranged for him to start at the hydrotherapy pool in January – I was really looking forward to that. We'd already taken him to an ordinary swimming pool, the one for little kids at Highbury. Wearing his waterproof nappy, he'd float about in an orange rubber ring, which had a seat and two holes for his legs. Pete's kids would take it in turns to tow him up and down the pool – he loved it, he was a proper water baby.

Life seemed to be settling into a regular routine, and as far as I was concerned, my own life was mapped out for the foreseeable future. I'd be at home with James, seeing to all his needs, and taking more and more pleasure in our beautiful boy – his developing personality, his heart-melting smiles (when he wasn't blanking me, of course) and, thank God, his increasing strength. As far as my acting was concerned, that was on hold, while Pete went on working at Television Centre as a studio resource manager. Between us, we'd take James for his regular clinic appointments at hospital. Family and friends would drop round, we'd have the odd day out ...

Then, out of the blue, I got a phone call from my agent. Granada TV were making a new series of the reality show *I'm a Celebrity, Get Me Out of Here!* – and would I like to take part?

No, I wouldn't. Apart from the fact that I was at home with James, roughing it in the rainforest wasn't my idea of fun. I'd only been camping once before, and that had ended in disaster and a festering foot. I'll stay in urban comfort, thanks. I'd seen previous series of the show – all bush tucker trials and climbing trees and eating kangaroo balls, as far as I could see. It's the sort of thing to watch through your fingers, cringing as so-called celebrities made idiots of themselves. All the horrible fascination of a car crash – without the real injuries, of course. There is that to be said for it.

I thought that was the end of the matter and got on with my life. But Granada rang again, and again. 'Oh, come on,' said my agent. 'It wouldn't hurt to meet them. And they've hoiked up the fee.' Oh really? I met them, there were more talks, all kinds of reassurances, and I thought it over, talked to Pete.

And I changed my mind. Why? First, and most importantly, James was so much better by now. If I went away for a while, it would be in the knowledge that he was stable and would be in good hands, chiefly his dad's. If I'd had the slightest doubt, I would never have considered it. Also, the TV people promised that in the unlikely event of anything adverse happening, I'd be on the next plane home.

Other reasons? What about raising my profile? Rising to a challenge? Testing my personal limits?

As if.

Imagine the interview. 'Tell me, Elaine Lordan, what was it that attracted you to the idea of being paid tens of thousands of pounds for two weeks' work?'

Hmmm, let me see …

Not that we were short of a few bob, but you never know what the future holds. I had no idea when I'd work again, and I wanted to make provision for James. The hefty sum of money they were offering would go a long way towards providing that. Besides, as Pete pointed out, even if I was offered acting work – a film part, say – I'd most likely have to be away on location for a lot longer than a fortnight, and the money would certainly be a lot less. All things considered, a stint in the jungle didn't seem such a mad idea after all.

Jumping ahead a bit, Pete told me that he and James were watching TV when I made my first appearance in the jungle. They were sitting with Julie and Tonny. 'Look, James, there's Mummy,' said Pete, pointing. Apparently James fixed his eyes on the screen, kicked his legs energetically and burst into peals of laughter. He just might as well have said, 'Look at her! What *does* my mum think she's doing?'

By then, I was asking myself the same question ...

CHAPTER TEN

Bungle in the Jungle

If I'd stayed in the hotel, I'd have been all right. As it was, me and the jungle did not get on. But I went there with good intentions – you sign up for something, you give it your best shot.

Naturally, there was quite a lot of preparation before we went out. I think this was the fifth series, so the TV people had got things pretty well organized by now. They sent us contestants sheets of paper with schedules and lists and recommendations. (By the way, when I say 'preparation', I mean the theory. As I was to find out, the practice put a different complexion on things.)

I looked at the list of clothes and equipment we'd be issued with once we got to the jungle. Backpack, shirts, trousers, water bottle … no surprises there. I'd be getting the boots in advance, apparently, so I could break them in. I could just see myself yomping round the wilds of Highbury.

Then I got to something on the list I'd never heard of.

'What's a modesty smock?' I asked Pete.

'A what?'

'A modesty smock – that's what it says here.'

'Well,' said Pete, 'I suppose it's a kind of smock … that you're modest in. Like on a beach, when people take their knickers off under a towel or something.'

Made sense. But the next entry didn't.

'Look at this,' I said to Pete. 'It says here one pair "protective gators".'

'What's wrong with that?' he said. 'Very sensible in the jungle, protecting your lower legs. You never know what you'll be treading in.'

'But it's not spelled G-A-I-T-E-R-S,' I said. 'It's spelt G-A-T-O-R-S – short for alligators! Do you think they'll be giving us a couple of crocs each? Like security guards?'

At least we could take our own underwear – oh, and as we'd be staying in a luxury hotel to start with, I needed to take something 'suitable' to wear. I suppose I had a few rags knocking around …

I was relieved to see that smoking wasn't forbidden, it being what was called a 'physical addiction' as opposed to a luxury (we were allowed one luxury each, too). Though, quite rightly of course, we had to be aware that there were rules about smoking on location – it's an ecologically sensitive area, so obviously we wouldn't be grinding our fag-ends into rare orchids or anything, or setting fire to the trees.

Anyway, I went through all the preliminaries – the fittings for clothes, the medical, and so on – and one fine November day there I was flying first class to Brisbane. Very nice too. Us contestants were put up in different hotels so we didn't know who our bush mates were going to be, before we all met up together. Mind you, there'd been the usual speculation in the press, so we had a pretty good idea. I'd heard on the grapevine that Sid Owen was taking part – I was over the moon! We'd worked together in *EastEnders*, and like me he'd left the show the previous year. What's more, he's an Anna Scher boy – we've always got on well, so there'd be at least one friendly familiar face.

I was staying in the Hyatt Hotel, which was absolutely beautiful. I had a front room that was bigger than my whole flat, a massive bedroom, two bathrooms, walk-in wardrobe, dressing-room space ... Fabulous. Though after the initial 'Wow!' it all felt a bit flat, to be honest. I was alone – all this luxury was a bit of a waste without Pete and James to share it with.

We also had chaperones – I hadn't had one of those since *Annie* days – whose job it was to keep us in their sight at all times in case the press got to us. I didn't quite understand this, though, as the paparazzi had been out in force already, and the Brit contingent had seen us off at Heathrow anyway. Still ...

I was in this lap of luxury for several days. All right so far. I rang Pete regularly, trying to remember the time difference, to let him know what he was missing, and to talk to James. On the morning of the big meeting, I wasn't exactly at my best, though. The previous night – well, four o'clock in the morning – my mobile had rung and woken me up.

My first thought was: emergency! But it turned out to be some idiot magazine journalist.

'You've woken me up!' I snapped at him. 'What the hell do you want?'

'Oh,' he said. 'I thought you'd be in the jungle now. I hoped we'd get an interview.'

'What? You thought we'd be in the jungle? Do you seriously think we're allowed to take mobiles into the jungle, you arsehole?'

I hung up. I was livid. I hate my sleep being disturbed and I couldn't get off again.

In the morning I tried to look wide awake, dolled myself up and went out to the Versace Hotel to meet the others on a terrace overlooking the water, in the bright sunshine. It was a really beautiful setting.

We entered the terrace one by one – as soon as I saw Sid I ran straight to him and gave him a hug. Then we all milled around, chatting, talking about the one luxury item we were allowed, nibbling at the food laid on and sampling the drinks. It was like being at a cocktail party – but you don't usually go off into the rainforest after one of those ...

I looked over at the other contestants. Oh my God! There's Jimmy Osmond! Little Jimmy Osmond, of the Osmonds fame. I'd loved him when I was a kid. His 'Long-haired Lover from Liverpool' was number one when I was about six – and it quickly became one of my party pieces, trotted out at the drop of a hat. He's not so little now, of course, but he has the same baby-faced charm, the same puppy-dog eyes. I recognized David Dickinson straight away, too, from the telly. As he looks like the love child of Peter Stringfellow crossed with a mahogany hallstand, you can't miss him – that's his own description, by the way. And there was another familiar face off the telly, Jilly Goolden, the wine expert.

At the risk of sounding like a cheesy compere, presenting ... more soap stars – Sheree Murphy from *Emmerdale*, and Kimberley Davies from *Neighbours*, who I think was the first Australian to appear on the show – wonder what put the others off? Plus a couple of singers, Jenny Frost, from Atomic Kitten, and Antony Costa, from boy band Blue. I hadn't met Antony before, but he made an immediate impression – a cross between a cheeky kid and an old-fashioned gentleman. Like Sid, a diamond.

Then there was Carol Thatcher. She can't help who her mother is, of course, but where I come from the name of Margaret Thatcher still provokes a knee-jerk reaction. Hatred, usually. Still, at first sight Carol didn't appear to be a chip off the old block, which could only be good.

After socializing, the ten of us got ready for our trip to bugland. We were kitted out in a kind of uniform – khaki jacket, bush hat, T-shirt with name printed on it, jungle trousers, rucksack ... we could have walked straight on to the set of *Crocodile Dundee*. Except Jimmy let the side down a bit. His luxury item was sticking out of his rucksack, highly visible. A fluffy teddy bear. Not very macho. In fact there'd been a few sideways glances – a grown man with a teddy bear? But, if you've seen the show, you'll remember just how useful that teddy would be.

My own luxury item might have been misinterpreted – a huge tub of Vaseline. It was actually for moisturising, enough to share with everyone. And I'd heard that if you spread it on the legs of the camp beds, bugs couldn't get a purchase on them and slid off – even more reason to have a lot of it.

The plan was to airlift us into the jungle by helicopter. I'm not very happy about flying as it is – something so very unnatural (to humans, anyway). Still, as I was to find out, if you're going to be up high, it's best to have metal all around you ...

We were divided into two groups – I was with Kimberley, Antony, Jimmy and Jenny – and we got into our respective helicopters, which swept dramatically off into the sky. Our pilot, a lovely bloke, said, 'Now I'm gonna scare you a bit.' And he did. Suddenly the two helicopters were flying parallel, then they did a huge dip down and peeled apart – it felt like we were flying upside down. A memorable experience. All the more so as the pilot received a message over the radio and we had to do it again. 'Sorry, folks,' he said, 'they didn't catch it first time.'

Finally, we flew straight along a ravine, then the two helicopters peeled off again and went their separate ways.

When we landed, we got ourselves together and found a map showing us where to go. After a false start – 'Where are you going, Jimmy?' – we trekked off into the wild, finding our way through the undergrowth shadowed by tall trees. Now, on screen this first bit of trekking looks as if it took about half an hour. It actually took hours and hours – and we didn't have any water. I began to feel distinctly shaky. Looking back, I think I'd seriously overestimated my level of fitness. I've always kept in shape – a legacy of my aerobics days – and not long ago I could have taken a trek like that in my stride, literally. But for some months things had been difficult. I'd been losing weight, and hadn't paid as much attention to diet and exercise as I should have. I know that sounds like an excuse for being a wimp, but I was really taken aback by how hard I found it. By now my heart was beginning to sink.

Reaching our first destination didn't make me feel better. Much worse, in fact, when I saw what was in store – we had to cross a ravine by means of a high wire. An 80-metre drop, they said. (I worked out that was over 250 feet – 250 feet!) I've never been good with heights, in fact I've been positively bad, avoiding them wherever possible. Talk about vertigo – instant recipe for panic attack. My legs collapsed under me, and my heart started pounding. No way could I get across that wire – even if there was a cable to hang on to and a safety harness.

The minute I saw it, I started to lose my nerve. It must have showed in my face, as I was aware at this point that the director was pointing to the cameraman and going, 'Close up.' That's right, get every twitch and tremble. I couldn't even stand up on the timber platform. 'You're joking – an 80-metre drop?'

We had to put the harness on without any help – all straps and buckles. I was useless to start with. I'm no good with gadgets at the best of times, and now my hands were shaking so much. I managed to get the bloody thing on eventually.

Who'd go first? We drew straws. Antony drew the short straw and off he went, with a 'Cheers, girls and boys.' What a trouper. I could tell he was a bit nervous, but he gave it a bloody good shot. He set the pattern for getting across, moving sideways, sliding his feet along the lower cable as he slid his hands along the upper cable for support. The harness was clipped on at two points. Things got tricky when you reached a junction and had to undo your harness one clip at a time to get over the obstruction. Antony made it nearly to the end before he slipped, dangling from his harness. But then he hauled himself up and got to the end – result! What a relief.

His way of getting across seemed perfectly logical, as much as anything did to me at this point, but most of us didn't realize there was a better way of doing it.

I was still sitting in a crumpled heap when Jenny started off. She's a feisty girl and set to it without even clipping her harness to the cable. Obviously the safety guys noticed this immediately, and then she crossed without too much trouble. Now it was Jimmy's turn, and he crossed confidently. I think he'd had practice in the Wild West. Then it was my turn. I stumbled on to the wire, clipped myself on somehow, and stood there shaking. The helicopter doing the aerial filming zoomed quite close for a good shot of the fear on my face, and I started shuffling sideways. The strength drained out of my arms, and now the wire was shaking as much as I was. I stopped. The others were yelling encouragement, which was nice, but didn't have any effect. Then I glanced down into the depths of the ravine – big mistake. Giddy, a rushing in the ears – my arms gave out and my feet slipped from the wire. I hung from my harness like a rag doll.

There were more shouts of encouragement. I could make out Antony's voice – 'Come on, Elaine, you can do it.' But I couldn't. I just about managed to gasp, 'Will somebody come and get me, please?' Well, no. Not for about twenty minutes, anyway, though it felt much longer.

By this time Kimberley had started on the wire, but was using a different stance. While we'd all stood – or in my case wobbled – sideways, she was facing forwards, placing one foot in front of the other, pointing her toes like a ballet dancer, just as she placed one hand in front of the other on the upper cable. Very strong and confident – I wished she'd let on about that technique a bit earlier. She couldn't get past me, of course.

'I can't stand here all day,' she told me.

'Sorry,' I said feebly. 'I'm very sorry.'

Eventually a guy came out and helped me back on my feet. He then stayed beside me, though I had to continue on my own, and eventually I managed to get to the other side. Where I collapsed in a heap, shaking and feeling sick.

No real time for a rest – we were off again, carrying our packs, still no water. I think that was cruel. Antony was great, though. He could see just how freaked out I was, and several times he said he needed to stop and rest, though it was me who needed the respite. I'd never felt so physically drained, I felt a hundred years old. I was the second oldest in the group, behind Jimmy, but he's really fit and healthy. We kept on trekking until I couldn't even manage to climb over little tussocks. I'd be on my knees, then sliding down the slope on my arse. All the time, of course, the camera crew were busy getting their footage, though I was grateful when we had to stop for them to run ahead of us to film from the front.

We were the first group to arrive at the camp – a clearing in the jungle, surrounded by tall trees, and, as we quickly realized, rocks with cameras poking out of them. I was pleasantly surprised to see that it was a pretty place, dinky and cosy, with camp beds laid out and a fire waiting to be lit. Fortunately it was lit pretty quickly, and I could use it to spark up my first fag (I'd been gasping). Then I flopped down on one of the beds. By now I'd realized I was totally out of my depth. The others were kind to me, saying I should just rest while they got on with their allotted tasks – collecting wood, putting a screen round the toilet, whatever. I felt exhausted mentally and physically. At that point I think I could have just slept for two weeks and then gone, 'Oh, is the show over now?'

Soon the other group arrived, with a lot of excited talk

about their trip. They'd parachuted down, in tandem with an instructor, which made me feel like a kid who hadn't got the best toy! I could have done that. Once you'd started you couldn't exactly turn back, and you were attached to somebody who knew what he was doing. Though I realize that sounds odd – being up 12,000 feet isn't as scary as being up 250 feet?

For the rest of the day people were settling in and getting their bearings, and I got chatting to some of them. I was delighted to find Jilly Goolden really good company, great fun. I just about fell in love with her when she let on that though she's not a smoker herself, she pretended she was – even smoking a fag on camera – so she could share out the ration of five a day that we were allowed. What a lovely lady! Unfortunately she'd picked menthol cigarettes, which aren't exactly favourite with us real hardened smokers. So she went into the bush telegraph hut, whatever it was called, and informed them that she wanted proper fags, thank you – and we got them!

And what about the arch-enemy's daughter? Carol Thatcher was just so good-humoured, down-to-earth – eccentric in the nicest possible way. Imagine getting into the nation's heart by weeing beside her bed at night, not caring if she was caught on camera. I couldn't bring myself to do it, though during the night I began to wish my luxury item was pull-up Snuggies (nappies, for those who don't know).

That first evening we had this really bland, boring food – rice and peas. But peas so hard they'd take your fillings out

– you could have used them in a pea shooter. Grumble, grumble – then Jimmy's teddy bear came into its own.

'I've stuffed my bear with salt and pepper,' he announced, pulling a sachet out of his bear's nether regions. There's a Boy Scout who's always prepared!

We all grabbed for the seasoning. I promptly overdid it in an attempt to make the food taste of something. But of course the Big Brother cameras caught Jimmy out and he was summoned to the bush telegraph to have his salt and pepper confiscated. As Carol said, 'That bear's got a flat arse and we have no seasoning.'

By now I was thinking that I really ought to get off my own arse and do something useful, so after dinner – if you could call it that – I wandered off into the jungle to gather firewood. And I passed out. I wasn't aware of what was happening – I felt sick and sweaty, my legs were trembling, then there was blackness. Apparently I was shaking uncontrollably and fell backwards. When I came round, I didn't know what the hell was happening. There was an oxygen mask on my face, and the medics who were kept on hand were telling me I'd fainted. I was bewildered – I'd never fainted in my life before.

Looking back, I've tried to reconstruct what happened next, but most of the memories are blurred. I'm not even absolutely sure about the sequence of events. I've tried looking through the souvenir DVD, fast-forwarding on occasion, and that rang some bells, but mostly it's a fog. I know I slept in a camp bed that night and pulled the covers up over my ears. I wanted to go to the loo, and that's when I wished I'd brought Snuggies in as my luxury item. And red dye on my legs! The trousers we'd been given to wear were red, but the dye obviously wasn't colour-fast. Good job the stains on my legs didn't look like blood – I'd have thought I was dying.

It must have been the next day, possibly the morning, and I know I'd been wandering round the camp. I passed out for a second time, and one of the things I do remember clearly was when I came round. It was surreal. I had an oxygen mask on, and there was Jimmy Osmond. All it needed was an angelic choir in the background and that'd be it – I really had died and gone to heaven.

Anyway, that was the end of my short and less than glorious stint in the jungle. The doctors were concerned, and thought I should get out of there. I was taken to hospital where I had tests. Fortunately everything was normal.

My own diagnosis is that it was exhaustion plus dehydration – along with the fact that I was nowhere near as fit as I thought I was. I can see now that for more than six months I'd been making huge demands on myself, just to keep going, thinking I could cope because that's what you have to do. My usual reserves, both physical and emotional, were empty. Of course, it wouldn't stop the press saying that I'd been drinking – yeah, right. I must have smuggled alcohol in my big tub of Vaseline.

The TV people really looked after me then. My agent,

Mario, flew out to keep me company, and we were put up in a beautiful house in Byron Bay for several days, while I was interviewed away from the press. I kept asking them why they'd been so keen for me to take part. 'I did tell you I was rubbish at camping and hated heights,' I said. 'You might have guessed I'd be useless.'

So what was my appeal? I suppose it would be pretty boring if all their contestants were superfit and got through every trial with no sweat and no drama …

*

I phoned Pete at the first opportunity and caught up on all the news back home. It turned out that the TV people had phoned him before I even appeared on screen in the jungle. Most of the show is pre-recorded and edited, so there's always a time lag, and of course there's the time difference itself, which is about ten hours ahead.

'They said they were phoning to pre-warn me,' Pete told me. 'They said you'd had a funny turn, you'd passed out, but I couldn't speak to you as they still hadn't decided whether you were going back in or not.'

As it happened, Pete had been in the pub with my dad when he took the call. Dad's partner Eileen had gone away for a while, and Sophie had been taking care of Dad in Stevenage. She'd brought him down to stay in the flat for a weekend. Dad's a proud, independent man, and Pete would look after him with tact and sensitivity – just as he had with Kevin when we were in Ireland for Mum's funeral. And it was great for grandad and grandson to see each other. James had been perfectly stable so far.

While Julie looked after James that day, Pete had driven Dad to the pub and escorted him in – he's pretty unsteady now, and needs help walking. It was a real treat for Dad. He still loves the pub as much as ever, more for the atmosphere, the social side, than the beer. And he's still a betting man. Doesn't take his eyes off the racing on the telly.

'When I got the call, I didn't want to upset your dad,' Pete explained, 'so I went out into the pub garden. When I got back I had to make out it was just some stuff about work, and your dad finished his pint quite happily.'

Then he told me how James had reacted when he saw me on telly. Everyone's a critic! The boy's got good judgement, though … and I did have the money to put by for him. Apparently Julie was a bit more sympathetic about my plight. When she saw me stranded on the high wire, apologizing to Kimberley and anyone else who might be listening for being in the way, she said, 'Look at her. She must be the only person stuck dangling eighty metres up in the air who still feels she has to say sorry …'

*

Looking back, it does make you wonder if things are meant to be. If I hadn't made such a balls-up in the jungle, I might have stayed on for a week or so. If I'd proved amazingly popular with the audience – a long shot, I know – I might even have stayed for two weeks. And that would have been time not spent with James. Time that could never be made up.

Time was not on our side.

CHAPTER ELEVEN

Farewell

Right, after that experience the only bush I'd ever go to again is Shepherd's Bush. You can keep the jungle. Give me city streets, hot and cold running water, a flushing toilet, proper food and all the other comforts of home. Talking of which – I couldn't have been happier when I was back in Highbury again and walking through our front door. I'm sure James greeted me with a bigger smile than usual. Had he missed me, or was he laughing at the memory of his mum on the telly?

It was so great to see him looking healthier and stronger now. It would be his birthday soon, on the 13th of December. In some ways this first year had flashed by, in other ways it had seemed to last for ever. So much had happened since James's birth. That first big operation to fix the diaphragmatic hernia, the follow-up procedures, the endless tests on one little precious body – our whole lives revolving round hospital, hoping for the best, fearing the worst. What a tightrope we walked! Then within a few months came my mum's shocking death, blasting all our lives, leaving such pain and regret. I was still holding myself in, trying to push the grief to the back of my mind. I knew it would come out some day, but not yet. Just now and then something would catch me – sorting out her flat, I'd find a note to me that she'd written but never posted, expressing such love and support, signing off as usual with 'Mam'. For a moment I'd be racked, but you have to pick yourself up, grit your teeth, wipe your eyes and carry on.

Throughout the year, as James's condition improved, the first glimmers of hope had grown into something approaching confidence. By November I knew I could leave him in safe hands for a while when I went off to the jungle. Not that we ever got complacent, Pete and me. We never took anything for granted. We took each day as it came, and at the end of each one, with James quietly asleep in his own cot, we thanked God – and the doctors and nurses – for another day with our son.

I can picture James now, a few days before his first birthday. There he is, sitting in his little chair by the fireplace – the one with the vibrating mechanism that he finds so soothing, and all the bells and whistles. His eyes are bright, his hair silky and he's kicking his legs just like any other healthy baby – he's worked out that if he kicks hard enough he can make the chair bounce about. He's laughing, showing two little teeth with more coming through, and holding a little cloth book in his hand. It's got pictures of a farm with animals and flowers in it, all made up of different textures he can touch – felt, and corduroy, that sort of thing. Some kind of crackly material is sewn into the pages, so he can make a loud noise with it, and there's a handy teething ring attached. He loves this book. Tonny, one of his godmothers, gave it to him. Julie, his other godmother, got a bit jealous and bought him a bigger, better one, but he never took to it. Touch of godmotherly rivalry there, I think – christening mugs at dawn!

Not that we'd had the actual christening yet. That was lined up for the new year, along with a ceremony to bless our wedding rings.

Ah yes. Pete and I had fixed a date for our wedding at last. We knew right from the start, years ago, that we would get married some day, when Pete's divorce came through. There just never seemed to be a hurry. And once James was born, organizing anything seemed out of the question, and after my mum's death we were hardly in the mood for celebration.

It was shortly after I'd got back from the jungle. We were sitting in the living room, looking at James in his chair, wondering out loud if it was safe to relax a bit. We'd gradually weaned James off his round-the-clock oxygen, and he only needed a smidgeon now and then – though of course he would need careful monitoring for the foreseeable future, until he was out of the woods entirely. Was it time to think about the two of us now?

Pete went down to Islington Town Hall and made enquiries.

'What date do you have in mind for your wedding?' he was asked.

'Soon as possible,' he said.

This turned out to be Thursday the 15th of December. We'd have a low-key ceremony at the town hall, just two days after James's birthday.

It might sound odd, but we didn't plan anything spectacular for James's birthday, either. It wouldn't exactly be just another day, but of course he could have no idea of its significance, and it's not as if he'd mixed with a lot of other babies who could be brought over to a party. For me and Pete, it was enough that he was still here, and thriving. Other parents might think of their baby's first birthday as a milestone, but every day had been a milestone for us.

As it happened, we did have a bit of a do. Lots of people sent cards, Sophie came round with a cake and balloons, and Julie, Kathy, Tillie and Tonny brought little presents. There's a lovely photo of James in his chair, laughing and looking up at the brightly coloured balloons above him. He's lifting his arms, trying to reach them, punch them into the air.

He was guest of honour at our wedding, dressed in a lovely new babygro that Julie had bought him, and a little cardi Tilly had given him – it had a cute hood with sticking-up ears. He sat in his pushchair, watching while his mum and dad tied the knot. Incidentally, the papers said that he was in a specially adapted pushchair with 'breathing tubes' – what? He never had a specially adapted pushchair. He'd always been in a regular pushchair, and by now didn't need his cannula and the portable oxygen cylinder 24/7. Where do these ideas come from?

We had a highly select guest list. As well as James, there was my sister Sophie, our cousin Kevin, and my friend Julie.

I tried not to think of how much Mum would have loved to have been there.

I must say the bride and groom looked very smart, if not exactly conventional. Pete wore black jeans and T-shirt with a dark jacket, and a red rose in his buttonhole arranged by Kev. I wore black bell-bottom flares slit way up the side, showing scarlet shoes with ribbons round the ankle and killer heels. I wore a dark top and a fluffy white bolero affair, and carried a little bunch of flowers, also arranged by Kev.

And we had a good day. The wedding might have been low-key, but it was a perfect, relaxed ceremony and we meant every word we said. James put in his twopenn'orth, too. When we got to the bit about 'Is there any reason why these two people should not get married … speak now …' – right on cue, James, who'd been observing proceedings quite placidly, suddenly yelled, 'Wa-a-a-ah!' We take this not as an objection to the marriage but his seal of approval.

The lovely people who had officiated in the town hall told us that there were photographers outside, and would we like to go out the back way? For once, we thought, why? This is our wedding day, and I, though I say it myself, was looking particularly gorgeous. So we went out into the winter sunshine, full of the joys of spring. There are pictures of Pete and me smiling fit to bust, me showing off my wedding ring – Pete had one, too, for the first time – showers of confetti from our guests, and a car (belonging to Julie) duly festooned with 'Just Married' signs and old cans – Coca-Cola, as it happened, arranged by Sophie, who liked to point out that it was the Real Thing. Very appropriate. As a finale Pete carried me not over a threshold, but over the zebra crossing outside the town hall.

There'd been another great photo opportunity, when I did the traditional bridal thing and threw my bunch of flowers up in the air behind me. The one who catches it is next to get married? Well, Julie had been standing by, on full alert – she was then without a Mr Right, so she moved forward and caught the flowers, much to her delight. Only to be floored by a rugby tackle from Kev – 'It's mine!' he cried, grabbing at the bunch. 'It's mine!' yelled Julie. 'Gerroff!' There was quite a tussle – Julie wasn't giving up those flowers easily, and she clutched them protectively to her chest while the pair of them fell about laughing.

Funny thing, though – Kev has since married his boyfriend Andrew in a civil ceremony, while Julie has yet to get hitched.

After the photos, we all went to a nearby bar for champagne and toasted each other. Then James, Sophie, Julie and Kev all went home for lunch, while Pete and I went off to one of our favourite local restaurants, where something happened that was as unusual as it was unexpected.

Halfway through our meal, this bloke turned up at our table and handed us a pile of photos.

'There you go,' he said. 'Your wedding photos.'

It turned out that he was a photographer on one of the major tabloids. God knows how he knew we were there, but he handed over the photos, very nice and polite.

'Do you want anything else?' we asked, rather taken aback at his show of generosity.

'No thanks,' he said, and off he went – no extra pics, no quotes. The photos were excellent quality, too, much better than ours. We'd just used throwaway cameras for the interior shots, but these professional ones were great. They'd go straight in the album – after we'd shown Pete's mum and sister. We planned to spend Christmas with Cath and Mike in their big house in Yorkshire, along with their four children and Pete's mum.

All in all, a memorable day. Happiest day of our lives.

*

James developed a slight cold the day after the wedding. We were well versed in what to do, and checked his sats. He needed more oxygen – so it went back on 24/7 again. There'd be an overnight study, and we'd send the monitor off to be analysed. We'd watch him throughout the day, and check his readings every half-hour. There was his baby monitor, too, so that we could hear him in the other room.

By Sunday morning, he still had a bit of a sniffle. Pete had to go to work, so James and I kept to our usual routine during the day. I put him to bed at about eight o'clock, and as I kissed him good night, he seemed perfectly normal. The cold symptoms weren't noticeable, and I checked on him half an hour later.

Something wasn't right. Was he lying too still? Was he even breathing? I remembered the CPR training we'd had.

It's easy to wake a sleeping baby with a gentle little nudge … I immediately tried, but he didn't stir.

He wasn't breathing.

For a split second I could hardly take this in, then I found the phone in my hand and I was dialling 999. An ambulance would come from the Whittington. That was the arrangement in case of any emergency. Remember the training, remember the training. Stay on the line – the operator would talk me through what to do. Oh God, we'd practised resuscitation just before James left hospital, six months ago, but I hadn't tried it since. That was it – off with the cannula and cover his nose and mouth with my mouth, and do quick short breaths into him – mustn't overdo it, mustn't overdo it. Put the phone down, pick it up, keep listening to the operator. Please, please, please, James, come on.

The ambulance arrived in moments, along with an ambulance car. The paramedics were all over James – they took charge. I tried ringing Pete, but his mobile was switched off. It would be, as he was working in the gallery. I could only leave a quick message. Now James was whisked into the ambulance. I wasn't allowed to go with him – they must have needed the room to work on him, so I followed behind in the ambulance car. We rushed along the streets, the siren wailing. I was vaguely aware of the blue lights flashing.

The last thing I remember clearly is phoning Julie – I must have someone with me, I must have someone with me. Then things happened in a blur. I remember only bits of the ambulance ride, getting to the hospital, sitting in the emergency treatment room while a team of medics stood over James as he lay on a trolley. The ambulance driver sat with me. He wouldn't leave, and that upped my anxiety. 'Don't you have to go out on another job?' I asked him. He shook his head. 'I'll stay,' he said.

I remember saying, 'He's going to die, isn't he?'

He said gently, 'Look, while they're working on him, there's still hope.'

Then Julie's here, her arms around me, she's saying something. The ambulance man is still sitting beside me. The medics are still clustered round the trolley. They're saying things to each other, passing each other bits of equipment. Where's Pete? Here he is at last, thank God.

We sit together, me, Pete, Julie and the ambulance man. I don't know for how long. I hear 'adrenaline' and something 'cardiac' coming from the medical team. I think someone makes a phone call. Suddenly another man comes into the room – he's clearly in charge and joins the team. There's a murmur of voices and a nodding and shaking of heads. Then all goes quiet and the people stand still. He comes over to us. 'I'm so sorry,' he says quietly. 'We've done everything we can …'

*

So that's why they summoned that new doctor. He was the one to 'call the death' – I think that's the right terminology. To establish that someone's died and to fix the time. Then there is the procedure.

'Would you like to dress him?' they ask.

We put him back in his babygro and Pete asks for a nappy – it would be odd if James didn't have one now.

'Do you want a lock of his hair?' someone asks.

'No thank you,' we say. 'Please leave his hair as it is.'

James lies there, looking perfectly peaceful, his eyes closed, his little face pink. I see the shadow of his amazingly long eyelashes on his cheeks. He could be asleep. I lift his eyelids – I'm not sure why. Perhaps I hope to see a flicker of life, even now. I hold him in my arms, breathing in his familiar smell. There's a little trickle of blood from his nose, which Pete wipes away.

I go to get Julie so she can say goodbye to James, then she leaves us. We hold him and cuddle him as if he was asleep.

Someone asks, 'Would you like a vicar or a priest?'

'Yes please, we'd like a priest.'

In what seems like no time, a priest is here, Father Voycek, who we've never met before.

'Our baby was going to be christened next month. Can you christen him now, please?'

'Of course,' he says. He has an American accent. He must be a visiting priest. There are prayers, beautiful words, and the sign of the cross on James's head.

'We were going to have our wedding rings blessed at the same time as he was christened. Can you do that for us too, please?'

'Of course.'

His words and prayers are so poignant as he blesses our rings over James's body. He seems to understand totally what we are going through, a truly spiritual person.

Then Father Voycek goes out, but leaves his rosary beads with us. They will become a memory of what he has done for us.

Then we are by ourselves with our son.

Kindly, we are asked, 'Do you want to sit with him all night? There's a room, you'll be private.'

All night? No, no thank you. 'I don't want to see him go blue!'

'He won't go blue, but he will go cold.'

Oh no, not cold. Not a cold dead face. I can't see my James like that. I must remember him as he always was – warm, and pink. I can't sit there and watch his little face lose its colour and go cold. I don't want that image to be the last I see of him. Just like my mum – I'll remember them both warm, and alive.

So Pete and I hold James for the last time. We stroke his face. We kiss him, again and again. And we finally say goodbye to our little fighter.

*

The first thing we had to do was phone our immediate family and friends. We stood outside A&E late on a cold rainy night, telling those who had loved James the most.

Then, sooner than you would expect, came the practicalities. First the police. Yes, the police. I can understand if that shocks you – our baby has just died and we're investigated by the police? Do they think we're criminals? How can they be so crass, so intrusive?

Yet, oddly enough, even at the time, one part of my brain registered that this was reasonable. The rest of my mind was in freefall – my chest and throat were hurting and my legs were trembling with shock, yet somehow I could work out what was happening and why. Of course. An unexpected death. An unexpected death could be a suspicious death. So the police have every right to be here.

Two nice officers talked to us at the hospital, and explained the procedure.

'We'll come home with you,' they said, 'and wait for the investigating officers from Scotland Yard.'

So we drove home, and the policemen followed in their van. In the rush to get to the hospital, I'd left the front door wide open. We went in, and Pete and I sat in the living room while one of the officers had a quick look over the flat. For all he knew, James's bedroom could be the scene of a crime and it had to be examined before anybody had a chance to alter anything, erase any evidence of wrong-doing. After all, everybody knows that some parents do awful things to their children. The police didn't know us, they didn't know that we weren't like that, they couldn't take anything for granted.

I think they were also checking for any obvious signs of neglect, like a dirty cot, or any evidence of smoking – anything that might have contributed to James's death. Pete and I both smoke, but after James was born we absolutely had a cast-iron rule of no smoking in the flat. We always went out into the back yard and closed the French windows. Still do.

When he'd finished, the officer said, 'I'll go and sit in the van with my colleague till the other officers arrive.'

On this cold night? 'Why don't you have a cup of tea?'

'Thanks, but I've got some calls to make.'

As it happened, he did pop in several times. We had to wait hours for the Scotland Yard officers – obviously they'd had to be woken up, then they had to get to the Whittington to see James and talk to the doctors …

So we sat with the policeman, chatting after a fashion. He said his wife was expecting their first baby. I looked at James's birthday presents still lying around the room, unwrapped but not used – he hadn't had much of a chance to play with them. I offered them to the officer and naturally he refused at first, but he could see that I just wanted some good to come from them so reluctantly he took them.

At last the Scotland Yard officers arrived, one woman and two men. They examined the flat, videoing and looking for any signs of concern. We could tell that they felt awful about what they were having to do. Very professional, of course, but sensitive, aware of how Pete and I must be feeling. We felt sorry for them, to be honest. What a horrible job – but one that in justice had to be done.

I can scarcely put into words how we were feeling – kind of suspended, numb. My brain was working, but emotionally I was empty. Pete felt the same. In any case, we had to hold ourselves together because the police were asking us all kinds of questions about James's medical history. Because we'd been so well trained in his care, and so practised, we had all the facts at our fingertips. Looking after him was second nature to us. It must have been obvious to the officers that we knew what we were talking about, that there were no suspicious circumstances.

Then they were leaving. 'Thank you very much,' they said again. 'You're doing very well, we have no concerns. There'll just be the formality of the post-mortem.'

Post-mortem – of course, for an unexpected death.

Pete and I were alone. The enormity of our son's death had been seeping in, all through the long hours while the police were here. We looked at each other. Something registered in my mind.

'It's so quiet,' I said.

'It's the oxygenator machine – it's turned off.'

The background humming we'd lived with for six months had gone.

*

Later on, much later on, I pieced together missing bits of the jigsaw, from what people told me. When Julie got my call, she dropped everything, as I knew she would. Her older kids are teenagers, they can look after themselves, but her youngest, Ellie, was only eight at the time. Julie woke her up and said she had to go over and stay at her nan's.

'Why?' asked Ellie.

Julie didn't say anything about James, knowing how upset Ellie would be.

'Elaine's not well, Pete's at work and she needs me. I need to go and look after her.'

Ellie could understand that. So Julie drove to Highbury, having phoned her mum in advance, and left Ellie there. She then went straight to the Whittington.

'When I got there,' she told me, 'I asked the person on the desk where was the baby that had just been brought in by ambulance, and they pointed to a room. I walked in, and saw you sitting there, next to an ambulance man. There was a crowd of people round a trolley – I realized they were working on James. I gave you a hug, and looked over your shoulder at the ambulance man. I mouthed, "Is he alive?" He shook his head and mouthed back, "I don't think so." I sat with you till Pete came.'

When Pete got the message he dropped everything and rushed to the hospital.

'I was just hoping I'd be in time,' he said. 'I had to force myself to concentrate on driving. It felt like my mind was split. I suppose I was hoping that you'd exaggerated James's condition, but when I got in that room I could see his little body clearly, with the team around him. Things didn't look good.'

We think the team had kept working on James until Pete arrived. Was it to show that they'd done absolutely everything possible to save our baby? But we would know that anyway. Pete reckons it might have been for both our sakes.

'Perhaps it was so I didn't just walk in and find him dead,' he says. 'So they could tell us both together.'

'Afterwards,' said Julie, 'I didn't know whether to stay or go.' I'd known she was torn. 'I wanted to be there for you – and I love James, so I wanted to be with him too – but I thought you and Pete would want to be by yourselves.'

The very next morning Tonny was on the doorstep, and stayed a couple of days. Tilly and Kathy arrived soon after, and again Kathy made her pot of wonderful soup – 'This must be the Death Soup,' I tried to joke. Eileen drove Dad down from Stevenage. Everyone was gathering.

The news spread. That week we'd had birthday cards, wedding cards and Christmas cards – now we had sympathy cards, too.

Such an outpouring of love for James. In his short life he seemed to touch everybody who met him – and I'm not just biased as his mum. People responded to his lovely little personality, his spirit, his tenacity. Everybody seemed to love him, they asked after him. And now they sent heartfelt messages of condolence.

One of the worst things was telling the children. They really loved James, and had learned to look after him. Pete drove over to his kids' house the next day and broke the news. They were devastated, in floods of tears. They couldn't believe it – like most kids, they associate death with old people, not little babies.

Children are so resilient, though. When the first shock dies down, they're still sad, of course, they take it in, and deal with it in their own way. Then after a while they ask questions. Why did he die? Where is he now? A few weeks after James died, Pete's younger daughter, then aged eight, had evidently been thinking. 'What is heaven?' she asked her dad.

Pete said it's not a physical place, it's a special place where your soul goes when you die ...

Her reply was, 'Oh, I thought it was the same as here, just in black and white.'

A monochrome heaven! She must have seen an old film or something to trigger that idea.

Julie had dreaded telling her younger daughter. Ellie had been so devoted to James. On the Monday Julie had taken her to school as usual and hadn't mentioned anything. She told her in the evening, and of course Ellie was devastated, just like Pete's children.

'She sobbed her heart out,' Julie told me. 'She was in pieces. I tried to soften it, somehow – I said, you know he hadn't been well ... but children don't expect babies to die.'

Ellie too showed that she was thinking about James's death. Some days later, she said to her mum, 'Perhaps James is happier now. He won't be in pain, will he? He won't need any more operations?'

'That's right,' said Julie.

*

We had to make sure people heard quickly – especially the children – because by the Tuesday the press had got hold of the news. That day I was lying in bed and there was a ring at the bell. Pete went to the door, and I heard a conversation. It was some strange woman. She gave her name and said that she was from such-and-such press agency, and, 'Can I speak to Elaine?'

Pete was incredulous. He said, 'Press agency? Press agency? You are joking, aren't you? You must realize what we're going through. Do you really expect us to talk to you at this time? Our baby died two days ago and you're here on our doorstep? Don't you have any respect for people's grief?'

He didn't shout and scream. As he always says, that doesn't achieve anything. But he made his feelings crystal clear, and the woman went away quite upset. Personally, I'm surprised they waited two days.

*

Another funeral to arrange. The Whittington sent James's body to Great Ormond Street for the post-mortem. The cause of death was formally ascertained as chronic lung disease. It seems that while James's health had generally been improving, the original damage to his lungs had been too extensive and they were under great stress.

This formality over, now his body could be released. We planned to have him cremated, at Islington Crematorium, but nothing could be done this side of Christmas. It would have to be after Christmas, and the date was set for Wednesday the 28th of December. Meanwhile James's body would rest in the funeral home.

We asked our local priest to officiate at the funeral. Father Willy had officiated at my mum's funeral, and it seemed fitting that he should do the same for her grandson. I've known him for quite a while – not so much from going to mass, but I do like to drop into the peace and tranquillity of the church now and then, light a candle, and have a chat.

As ever, Father Willy was kind and understanding, and very practical. We knew the arrangements would be safe in his hands.

At first we felt it should be just us, Pete and me, saying goodbye to James. But of course all those he had touched in his short life wanted to be there. These included not only our close family and friends, but those nurses and medical staff who had cared for him, as well as other parents we'd got to know in the intensive care unit, and the people from the Child Development Team who had tried so hard to make James better.

We used Miller's, the funeral directors who had so sympathetically organized Mum's funeral. We told them that we would need just the one hearse, to come to the flat, and a few of us would travel with him to the crematorium.

The kind man said, 'I'm afraid your son may need to travel in a separate hearse, as he's over a year old. So the coffin will be bigger than a little baby's.'

'You haven't seen him yet,' we said. 'When you do, you'll be surprised. He's quite small and if we can we would like to go with him in the hearse, if possible.'

We didn't want a large crowd coming to the flat, and us

all going in procession, so we asked our family and friends to meet us at the crematorium – even Dad. With his worsening condition, I didn't want him struggling in and out of cars.

We asked for no flowers, but donations in lieu to go towards a new scanning machine for the unit at UCLH. We had asked for some simple white roses to go on top of the coffin.

Those arrangements taken care of, now there was just Christmas to get through. Should we go ahead with our original plan to go to Yorkshire, to see Pete's mum and his sister and her family? When we planned it, we were thinking of a real family Christmas for James – he'd be with his mum and dad, his nan, his aunt and uncle and his four cousins. We'd all have a lot of fun. Now we drifted around the flat, seeing James's things everywhere. It was so odd not to see him here, where he belonged. I kept looking at his little chair by the fireplace, forcing it into my head that he'd never be there again.

In the event, Pete's sister urged us to come, so we did go north. I felt at the time it wouldn't make much difference where we went, but in fact it was a good decision – Pete's family are so warm and hospitable, so understanding.

We came back home on the Tuesday after Christmas, the day before the funeral. We went round to the church house to see Father Willy, as we had some changes to make to the service. Pete had asked his mum and sister to suggest some prayers and readings.

To our surprise, instead of Father Willy, Father Voycek opened the door.

'How lovely to see you again!' we said. 'We didn't even know you lived here.'

'Yeah, I live here,' he said, beaming at us. 'Father Willy is out right now, visiting some folks, but I'm more than happy to help if I can. Come in, come in.'

Then he said the oddest thing I've ever heard a Catholic priest say.

'Come and smoke with me in my tepee.'

What?

He wasn't kidding – well, it was a room rather than a tepee, but the walls and surfaces were covered in ethnic-style cloths and American Indian artefacts. The designs looked familiar, and I suddenly realized why.

'You were wearing a stole with designs like those,' I said, 'when you christened our son.'

'Yeah, sure was,' said Father Voycek.

It turned out that he was Canadian rather than American, and had close ties with Native American communities. He said he liked to think of himself as one of them. He even had a brother – I'm not sure if they're still called blood brothers – called Big Buffalo. He was immersed in their culture, and liked to have reminders of it wherever he went.

He offered me and Pete cigars – standing in for a pipe of peace, I suppose.

'Thanks, but I don't smoke cigars,' I said, having a sudden flashback to my mum being offered a cigar by Pete. She was obviously bolder than me!

'You'll have a drink, though,' said Father Voycek.

So me and Pete found ourselves sitting cross-legged on the floor of Father Voycek's makeshift tepee, smoking fags and drinking Jack Daniel's.

And, believe it or not, it was one of the most spiritual experiences we've ever had.

'Thank you so much for what you did for James last week,' we began. 'It was absolutely beautiful …'

And we talked, all of us, about – well, anything and everything. Father Voycek was so intuitive, so responsive, so understanding. Then he said a wonderful thing. We were thanking him yet again for his support, and he broke in with: 'But you've given me strength, by your strength – I've learned so much from you.'

Well, that gave Pete and me such heart. We felt more able now to face the next day, and asked Father Voycek if he would join Father Willy in conducting the funeral.

'I'd be honoured,' he said. He'd christened James, now he would help perform the final ceremony.

*

It was a bright, sunny, winter morning, cold and clear. Pete and I waited in the flat, along with my sister Sophie, Julie, Tonny, Kathy and Tilly. The people who had known James so well, and looked after him with such devotion, who had truly been part of his life. They'd go with him now.

The hearse arrived, and we took our places. As we'd known, a baby coffin was right for James, and it lay in the front of the hearse. Kathy sat beside it, keeping it steady. The rest of us sat in the back.

We arrived at the crematorium, where everyone else was waiting. Pete carried the little white coffin from the hearse into the chapel, through the doors and down the aisle, and placed it on a dais, like a little altar, with curtains on either side.

It was such a wonderful service, conducted with grace by Father Willy and Father Voycek. We sang 'All Things Bright and Beautiful'. Pete's mum had asked for a special prayer, which I read out. His sister had asked for another, which Tonny read out. There were informal words, too, precious memories, which touched us all to the heart.

We'd asked for a special song to be played at the end, while everyone was leaving, but Father Willy had had an inspired idea.

'Elaine and Pete have asked for a final song to be played as you leave, but it's so touching that I think everybody should stay and share in it.'

As the music ended, Father Willy said, 'Now we will all go, and leave Elaine and Pete alone with James.'

So we stayed there in the chapel, our hands on the coffin, saying goodbye. We'd asked for the curtains to stay open – I hate it when they close and you know the coffin is gliding off. So as we left, they were still open.

It was over. Most of the guests went on their way, with many expressions of love and support. Eileen drove off with Dad. Just a couple of people came back to the flat, but not for a wake. We just sat around and talked. We all had our little stories about James. For someone who'd lived for just over a year, there was a lot to say! Such special memories – and laughs too.

We decided not to bury James's ashes under a headstone. I know some people derive comfort from giving their loved one a final resting place, somewhere tangible that they can visit, but Pete and I don't think like that. For us it's all about remembering the life. So we were just going to wait until something seemed right.

*

It was a few months later, by which time I'd picked myself up a bit. After the funeral, I don't remember a lot. Pete reckons that all the grief for my mum that I'd kept bottled up finally came to the surface when James died, and burst out. I was grieving for two people I'd loved with all my heart, and my heart was breaking.

Anyway, when I was more myself, we carried out our last plan for James. His ashes had been kept at the crematorium, until Miller's collected them. They'd kept them until we were ready. We hadn't known what to do with them – sprinkle them in the garden? Highbury Fields? No – that didn't seem right. Then we thought of the first time we'd met.

So we took his ashes to Brighton, where Pete and I had met five years before. We stayed in the same hotel overnight, and in the morning we went down to the beach just outside. It was late March, and the weather matched our mood. It was damp, and a mist hung in the air. The beach was deserted. This is where we'd say our farewell to our son.

We stood for a while, our tears mingling with the damp. Then we walked down the shingle to the water's edge, and paddled in a little way. We took the top off the urn, and took it in turns to take out some of the ashes.

Each time a wave came in, we threw more of the ashes on to the water, each wave taking them out to sea. Then there was just a little left. Together we flung the last ashes into the sea – and wouldn't you know it … a huge wave came out of nowhere and drenched us. As we staggered back, one thought flashed through both our minds. James – trust you to have the last word!

And as so many times when he was alive, we could only laugh and cry.

EPILOGUE

What More Can I Say?

I'm coming to the end of the story I've wanted to tell. It was death that prompted me to think so much about life. I hope I've done my mum and my son justice.

I think I feel a bit easier in my mind – catharsis, isn't it? Letting go of all the emotions you've had to keep pent up while you got on with life. Certainly the first raw pain has lost its edge. And every time a memory makes me cry and feel bereft, another makes me laugh and feel such warmth.

Not that you can exist on just an emotional level. Anyone who's been bereaved knows that there are lots of practicalities to attend to – the funeral, of course, trying to follow what you think would be the wishes of your loved one, while attending to the feelings of your family and friends. A lot of people say that having all these things to do concentrates the mind in the first awful days. It's a helpful function at the time. Most people seem to go through it in a state of suspension, waiting till the formalities are over before letting down their defences. For us, one shred of comfort during my mum's funeral was seeing how well loved she was by everybody – standing room only in St Joan of Arc's.

When we came back from Mum's funeral in Ireland, we couldn't face the other formalities straight away. Paperwork. Telling the pension people, the insurance people. The utilities. All the practical stuff. And sorting out Mum's flat – we didn't rush into that. Sophie and I took our time, when we felt up to it (and, of course, I had to fit it around the time I was spending at the hospital with James). Mum had been right in the middle of things, so it took a long time to sort everything out – clothes, paperwork and the eventual selling of the flat.

We kept some precious mementos, for ourselves and other close family and friends, and found good homes for her other belongings. She had such nice things, and she'd have been the first to insist that they went to people who would appreciate them. There was some small comfort in that.

So we could cope with these formalities, after a fashion, after a while. What was weighing heavily – and was outside our control – was the inquest. I may have been told just why it had to take nearly a year to happen. If so, then I've forgotten. But it was a long time coming. It finally took place on the 8th of March 2006.

I couldn't bear to go. Not just because I was in such a state, but also because I was scared that the press would intrude and turn it into a circus. It's one thing to have press attention at a wedding – when we got married, it was a laugh – but an inquest on my mum's sudden death ... please, no. It turned out that I'd made the right decision, as there were photographers hanging around.

The inquest was held in St Pancras Coroner's Court. Dad and Sophie went, and Pete went with them. As Pete told me, Sophie bravely spoke up in court, expressing our belief that Mum didn't intend to commit suicide – she was so distressed, so disorientated, by her chronic lack of sleep, that she couldn't have been thinking straight. She couldn't have known what she was doing. Sophie stressed that if Mum had been given the appropriate medical help, she would be alive today.

Various other people gave their testimony, including the tube driver, of course – I know Mum would have sympathized with any distress he'd been caused.

In the event, it took the jury only an hour to give their verdict: Mrs Bernadette Lordan took her own life. That seemed to be it. No other comment.

*

While thoughts of Mum are always in the back of my mind, sometimes they get jerked to the front, so to speak. I've come to realize that anything – the simplest everyday occurrence – can remind me of her and bring home how much I miss her. Especially at Christmas. I'd pop into Marks & Spencer, and when I saw all the people buying their special party food, I'd think, that's what she should be doing now. She should be piling her trolley high, making meals for the 5,000 again – what a wonderful hostess she was.

It's over a year now since James died, and I can't say that Pete and I think about him more at certain times of year than we do anyway. By now, we've given away a lot of his things. I know some people can't bear to do this, even going so far as keeping a special place in the home, a kind of shrine. I'm the last person to say what anyone should do to bear their grief, but that way isn't mine and Pete's. In fact the only item we've kept is the little cloth book that James loved so much, the one with the textures and the crackly filling. If I press the book to my nose, I can still smell him.

We have a few other things in storage. We have masses of photos, of course, displayed all round the flat and stored in albums. All the stages of James's life from his very first day, with all the people who loved him so much.

We only have one small snippet of James on video. We never filmed him much. We kept meaning to, and I know most people do loads if they can. I don't know, something stopped us. Now we think it might have been some buried defence mechanism. If we had lots of film of him moving, smiling, waving to us – perhaps we wouldn't be able to tear our eyes away. We'd sit in front of the telly obsessively soaking up every movement, every expression – yearning to reach out through the screen and touch him. Such a convincing image of life. Perhaps deep down, with our fear of losing him, that's why we didn't take that step.

Photos, though, are static. A single moment captured, but triggering off so many memories, so many associations. We can walk through the flat, and if one of James's pictures happens to catch the eye – well, we stop and look at it, pick it up perhaps, and smile.

As I say, this is just our way of seeing things. Everybody has to reach a place that's right for them.

I realize now that a lot of James's story has been about the things that were done for him. We look at it the other way round – what he did for me and Pete and other people.

The first thing he gave me, of course, was the experience of being a mum, feeling that pure, undiluted, unconditional love for one person. I've been on the receiving end, as a daughter (and still am), but when James was born, I was privileged to feel it for him. Pete was already a father, of course, so he'd had experience of it. What an immeasurable blessing.

James touched so many hearts. And he taught his mum and dad so much. We learned the value of patience, learned to adapt to the technological demands of his condition – learned what we were capable of, in short. What's more, through our experience of intensive care, we realized that many babies and young children are even worse off, and that their parents have far more to bear than we did. We were always so impressed by their courage and fortitude. Our experience has made Pete and me more understanding, and sensitive to what other people have to endure.

Most of all, perhaps, James inspired us to realize just how precious life is, however long it lasts. Young as he was, he had a great personality, he was an utterly lovable, individual spirit. His smiles, his laughs, rocking in his little chair … Even with everything he went through, he still seemed to enjoy life, and we wouldn't have been without him for the world. Just as I wouldn't have been without my mum.

For all the pain of losing them, nothing can take away the joy of knowing them, loving them, even if their time was cut short. That's what I've held to. It's helped me get through the worst times. Now, I think, I have managed to get back on my feet again, after a fashion. It's just a different life from what it would have been if Mum and James were still here. But whatever that life holds for me, I know they'll be with me, in my mind and my heart. Always.